CRUCIFORM

Living the Cross-Shaped Life

Jimmy Davis
Cruciform Press | Released April, 2011

Christine: The way you live—denying yourself
daily, taking up your cross, and faithfully
following Jesus—paints a God-glorifying portrait of
the Cruciform Life.
Abi, Micah, and Anna: I'm praying that you will
learn, love, and live the cross-shaped life.
Remember, Jesus loves you, and so do I.
– Jimmy Davis

CruciformPress

"Jimmy Davis loves the cross. This little book will open your heart up to see how the cross is the center of all of life. Well done."

Paul Miller, Director of seeJesus.net, author of *A Praying Life*

"In our day, when all kinds of words are being tossed around to describe the faith of Christ, we need some down-to-earth sanity to help us sort out what it really means to be a Christian. What better image than that which Jimmy Davis supplies in the cross of Jesus Christ? The Christian is a temple of the Lord, a cathedral devoted to demonstrating the power of the cross. Jimmy explains to us how this ancient image, first endorsed by our Savior himself, is the best way—and, really, the only way—to think about the life to which we've been called as Christians. With sound biblical exposition, clear and helpful illustrations, and a wealth of practical guidance, Jimmy Davis shows us how to cut through the fog of contemporary Christian thinking to recover the Savior's plan for our lives."

T. M. Moore, Dean of Chuck Colson's Centurions Program, Principal of the Fellowship of Ailbe, author of *Culture Matters*

"In *Cruciform: Living the Cross-Shaped Life*, my friend Jimmy Davis compellingly demonstrates that the gospel is just as necessary and relevant after you become a Christian as it is before. Jimmy shows from personal experience how a lack of passion and purpose, focus and fervor, compassion and conviction, is always due to distance from the now-power of the gospel. I pray that through this book you will rediscover the beauty and brilliance of the gospel in brand new ways."

Tullian Tchividjian, Senior Pastor of Coral Ridge Presbyterian Church, author of *Surprised by Grace: God's Relentless Pursuit of Rebels*

"*Cruciform* is a theologically grounded and redemptively freeing picture of a life spent boasting in the cross of Jesus. Avoiding the distortions of both repressive legalism and irresponsible antinomianism, Jimmy Davis helps us understand how the indicatives of God's grace lead to the imperatives of obedient love. This book will help many people understand what the gospel driven life is all about."

Scotty Smith, Pastor for Preaching, Christ Community Church, Franklin, Tennessee

"*Cruciform* is built on sound theology that has been tested in the crucible of life and found to be true. This book will be a help to everyone struggling with "Why, God?" As a seminary professor, I believe every person planning for, and serving, in a place of Christian ministry should read this book."

Dr. Brian Richardson, Basil Manly, Jr. Professor of Christian Ministry, The Southern Baptist Theological Seminary

"In today's evangelical culture, the cross of Christ is a no-show in many churches and sermons. Not in Jimmy Davis' *Cruciform: Living the Cross-Shaped Life*. The Cross is not merely a message, he says, it forms the template and the substance of how we live, worship and disciple. Chock full of memorable stories, illustrations, and Scripture, this is a terrific book for those breakfast discipleship groups. It is the next one I am going to use."

Dr. William E. Brown, President, Cedarville University

"The cross-shaped life is a life that's larger than life, far wider, deeper, and higher than we can possibly imagine. If the gospel has become at all routine to you or you simply wish to be freshly amazed at the transformative grace of God to you in Christ Jesus, read Jimmy Davis' book *Cruciform: Living the Cross-Shaped Life*. In it, Jimmy provides stunning, gospel-saturated vistas of what a cross-shaped life looks like in real life. If you are like me, you will want to read it more than once. It's that spiritually helpful."

Dan Cruver, Director of Together for Adoption and editor of *Reclaiming Adoption: Missional Living Through the Rediscovery of Abba Father*

"Jimmy Davis helps us understand that the cruciform shape of history and our living is the only way to make sense of both. He leads us to see that the death of Christ is not only something done for us but also something done in us. And he helps us to see that the cruciform life is the most practical one of all."

Dr. Joseph (Skip) Ryan, Chancellor and Professor of Practical Theology, Redeemer Seminary, Dallas

"Jimmy Davis has developed a simple but profound approach to the Christian life using the symbol of the Cross. The three elements in the shape of the cross—vertically, our love for and from God; horizontally, our love to and from others; and the intersection and unity of these two directions—pack a powerful punch."

David Arthur, Executive Vice President, Precept Ministries International

"With compelling stories, winsome humor, and sound theology, Jimmy Davis draws us into the power and purpose of our lives revealed by our cross-shaped story. Read this book to know and grow in a life of radical discipleship. Read this book to see how your Cruciform life reveals God's grace and glory to a broken and desperate world."

Elizabeth Reynolds Turnage, author, *Learning God's Story of Grace*

"In *Cruciform: Living the Cross-Shaped Life*, Jimmy Davis calls us to live beyond what comes naturally and live into lives truly shaped by the cross. In a world habitually turned in on itself, this book speaks a word we desperately need to hear: a word about life so anchored in Christ that our lives and our ministries can't help being transformed as a result."

Mark DeVries, author of *Family-Based Youth Ministry*, Associate Pastor for Youth and Their Families, First Presbyterian Church, Nashville

Table of Contents

Print ISBN: 978-1-936760-14-5
ePub ISBN: 978-1-936760-16-9
Mobipocket ISBN: 978-1-936760-15-2

CruciformPress.com
email: info@CruciformPress.com
Facebook: http://on.fb.me/Cruciform
Twitter: @CruciformPress
Newsletter: http://bit.ly/CruciformNL

Published by Cruciform Press, Adelphi, Maryland. Copyright © 2011 by James B. Davis, Jr. All rights reserved. Unless otherwise indicated, all Scripture quotations are taken from: The Holy Bible: English Standard Version, Copyright © 2001 by Crossway Bibles, a division of Good News Publishers. Used by permission. All rights reserved. Italics or bold text within Scripture quotations indicates emphasis added.

Illustrations by Denton Lesslie www.dentonsdesigns.com

INTRODUCTION

Cruciform Cathedrals

Those grand and glorious cathedrals built in the Middle Ages may have something to teach us about the way we live the Christian life today. The medieval church ministered to a culture that had no direct, personal access to the Scriptures in their own language. The church leaders of that era were faced with the challenge of teaching biblical truth to a Bible-less people. One creative way they taught key doctrines was by building object lessons into their church facilities. The cathedral served as "The Poor Man's Bible," as historians now call it. Everything about the way a cathedral was built—firm foundations and transcendent towers, storytelling statues of stone, tile mosaics and stained glass windows depicting central biblical stories in full color, and even the way sunlight streamed through those windows—was designed to help folks discern, delight in, and declare the great, biblical doctrines concerning God and the gospel.

The art and architecture of these sanctuaries taught two central biblical truths: God's just judgment against the sinfulness of mankind; and God's gracious provision of salvation from his wrath through the life, crucifixion, and resurrection of Jesus Christ. Cathedrals were intentionally built to teach theology to the people in the pews. And not just random bits and pieces of biblical teaching, but a consistent curriculum of repentance from sin and faith in Jesus as he is offered in the gospel. Indeed, the most distinct feature of these cathedrals was their *cruciform* or "cross-shaped" floor plan. *The central doctrine the church building communicated was the gospel, the message of the cross.* And since these church buildings were the most prominent and prized buildings, the hope was that through the preaching of the gospel inside the church building and through the presentation of the gospel in its art and architecture, the surrounding population would both see and hear the message of the cross.

We Need More Cruciform Cathedrals

Here in the 21st century we need more cruciform churches. Not lavish cathedrals but living communities of disciples being shaped *by* the cross into the shape *of* the cross for the glory of God and the good of our neighbors, the nations, and the next generation. Our best hope is to cooperate with The Architect, who promised he would build his church (Matthew 16:18) as we join him to form our families, small groups, and churches into "cruciform communities." Such communities visibly show and verbally share the message of

8

the cross because they are made up of people who have been vibrantly shaped by that message.

Cruciform Christians and Cruciform Churches

Unlike the cathedrals of the Middle Ages, this construction project requires both a cruciform building and cruciform building blocks. The Apostle Paul taught that both our individual bodies (1 Corinthians 6:19) and the corporate Body of Christ (1 Corinthians 3:16-17) are temples in whom the Spirit and glory of God dwell. The biblical blueprint calls for Christians and churches to live what I'm calling "the Cruciform Life."

So grab your work gloves, strap on your tool belt, and put on your hardhat and safety glasses. Let's partner together with the Architect as he builds his cruciform cathedrals in and with us.

One
CREATED TO BE CRUCIFORM

It started in fourth grade when my buddy Tommy and I entered our class talent show. Elvis had died that summer, so with all the taste, compassion, and sensitivity of 10-year-old boys we decided to pay tribute to the King by mocking him. I sang "Hound Dog" while Tommy ran around on all fours, barking. We were a hit.

By fifth grade my family had moved, so I decided to bring Elvis back for the all-school talent show. This time it was serious—out with the canine sidekick, in with the costume. My mom slaved over a sewing machine to tailor a white jumpsuit, complete with rhinestones, high collar, and giant belt buckle. My dad squeezed half a tube of goo into my hair and combed it into an impressive pompadour. I took that stage and stole the hearts of the grade-school girls and their moms. "Jailhouse Rock" and "Love Me Tender" never sounded so good, *thankyouverymuch*, and I became known as "The kid who does Elvis."

Seventh grade brought yet another new school. Since my older brother was already established there, I was mostly known as "Jeff's little brother." But that changed when I showed up at the Homecoming banquet in full Elvis mode. As everyone applauded and the Homecoming Queen planted a kiss on my cheek, I basked in the attention. I had made a name for myself. From then on in that school, I was "Little Elvis."

Why do I offer this odd glimpse into my past so early in the book? Because as any good theologian will tell you, Elvis impersonation has its roots in the Garden of Eden.

We are all born to *be someone special*; all created to *do something special*. Indeed, we were made to partner with God's community and participate in his mission. But one way or another we all tend to pursue a people and a purpose that neither relies on nor revolves around God. We have this desperate, unshakable need to be special, but that need gets misdirected, so we find ourselves in a kind of costume, pretending to be someone we are not meant to be and singing songs that are not really our own.

Pastor Tullian Tchividjian offers a brief explanation for how we came to this condition. "Essentially, the Bible tells a three-part story. *Creation:* God made everything good. *Fall:* Our sin has broken everything. *Redemption:* Everything in Christ will be made new."[1] That is an excellent summary of what's gone wrong and how God will make it right, but to really understand how Elvis impersonation and our countless other strivings for human greatness relate to Adam and Eve, we need to go a little deeper.

Creation

The first words on the first page of the first book of the Bible are, "In the beginning, God created." That is the right anchor point for the story of creation, but another passage in the Bible actually looks further back. Writing after the resurrection of Christ, the Apostle John's New Testament account of the story of Jesus opens with, "In the beginning was the Word."

John was present among the disciples on Resurrection Sunday when Jesus "opened their minds to understand the Scriptures" as being all about him, their long-awaited Messiah (Luke 24:45). Moses wrote Genesis 1 to describe creation, but when we talk about origins from *this* side of the resurrection, we must go further back. We must begin where John began.

In the Beginning Was a Community on Mission

John 1:1-15 gives us a glimpse into the eternal plans of God. It is the prequel to Creation because God's story really begins with himself. It begins with the God who is a three-in-one community: "and the Word was with God, and the Word was God. He was in the beginning with God" (John 1:1). The community we understand as the Trinity was there in the beginning, with each member participating in creation (Genesis 1:1-2, John 1:2-23, Colossians 1:16, Hebrews 1:2). The story begins with God's mission to show his glory and goodness by sharing with his creation the overflow of the fullness of his grace and truth.

God's story begins with *the* Community on *the* Mission.

God Created a Community on Mission

Genesis 1 and 2 teach something affirmed by John: God is a being intent on doing. In fact, God began his doing with a unique special project: he created the heavens and the earth and filled them with unfathomable radiance and resources (Genesis 1:1-25). But he didn't stop there. This triune God was on a mission to build a people in his image, created for his glory (Genesis 1:26-28, Isaiah 43:7). Adam and Eve were made to relate and to create, just like the inherently communal and creative God who made them. They were created in the image of God for relationship as his beloved son and daughter and also rulership as his blessed servants.

When God made mankind he created a people with a purpose, sons who would serve. They were not only meant to take delight in one another, but also to take dominion over all that God had made (Genesis 1:28). As his "kingdom of priests," the mission of God's son-servants was to "work and keep" creation, to cultivate and care for the place in which he put them so that it would be the dwelling place of God and his people, for the glory of God and the good of others forever (Genesis 2:15; Numbers 3:7-8; Exodus 19:6; Revelation 1:6, 5:10).[2] If God is a relationship that rules, a being who is doing, those made in his image and likeness must also relate and rule. Each human being is designed for relationship—to *be someone special* to God and to one another—and for rule, as together they *do something special* for the glory of God and the good of all God has made.

Created to Be Cruciform

We too were made to live in God's community and on God's mission. We were made for *God*, for *people*, and for *creation*. The stick-figure diagram below illustrates what I mean. Like Adam and Eve, we were made to live in right, loving relationship with God, people, and all that God has made (Genesis 1:26-28, 2:15-25). We exist and have been placed here *for* God, *for* other people, and *for* the sake of all creation. We exist to exalt the glory of God and to help other people and all of creation do the same (Psalm 8, Isaiah 43:6-7).

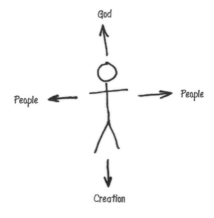

In my family, this is what we call living with a you-first heart. We were created to look away from ourselves toward God, other people, and all of creation and say, "You first." A person with a you-first heart recognizes that life is about using oneself to serve God, others, and all that God has made, thus living a life that takes the form of a cross. Can you see it? We were created to be cruciform (*cruci* = cross, *form* = shaped). Like Adam and Eve, we were made to live a cross-shaped life.

Fall

Today, however, cruciform is not the norm. A quick look at the way we and others fulfill our various relationships, roles, and responsibilities tells us we're not in Eden anymore. Something has gone terribly wrong. The people God made became a *man-centered community* on *man's mission* to multiply *man's glory* for *man's good* throughout all creation forever. Since then, people no longer live with you-first hearts but lean toward living with me-first hearts.

This drawing represents the human condition as we know it. People are disconnected from God, isolated from one another, and cut off from meaningful purpose in the world. The arrows are broken because our relationships with God, people, and creation are broken. The arrows point inward, indicating that we have traded the self-sacrificing cruciform life for the self-centered life of a me-first heart. Rather than using ourselves to serve God, people, and creation, we live to use God, people, and creation to serve ourselves.

The Story Has a Villain

What happened? How did we all become isolated individuals who live for our own glory and good? In Genesis 3 we're introduced to one who hates God's community and God's mission. The serpent that slithered his way into God's garden is "that ancient serpent, who is called the devil and Satan, the deceiver of the whole world" (Revelation 12:9). The Adversary sought to disassemble God's new community and distract them from their mission (Genesis 3:1-5). Satan suggested that perhaps God was not as open to share his community and mission as Adam and Eve had first believed. Adam and Eve listened to these lies and came to think there was something better than that which God offered them. This was an illusion, yet they wanted it. They wanted to do it their way. So they traded their you-first hearts for me-first hearts. God's son-servants rebelled against their Father, the

King. They rebelled against the being and doing of God, and thus lost their passion for and place in God's community and God's mission.

The Brokenness Begins

Adam and Eve's broken relationship with God led to broken relationships with one another and with creation. This unraveled their relationships with God's people and purpose as well. Genesis 3 describes their alienation and aimlessness.

First, their *relationship with God* was broken. They once enjoyed unhindered partnership with their Creator and participation in his creative work, but having disobeyed his Word, they became disconnected from him (Genesis 3:8-11).

Second, their *relationship with people* was ruined. What was once a beautiful partnership of oneness (Genesis 2:18-25) disintegrated into furious finger-pointing (Genesis 3:12). Disobedience to God left them distant from and divided against one another (Genesis 3:7).

Finally, their *relationship with creation* was corrupted. They retained their created purpose to *be someone special* by becoming an intimate community, but their efforts to do so would often seem futile (Genesis 3:16). They retained their created purpose to *do something special* by pursuing a God-given mission, but their plans would regularly be frustrated (Genesis 3:17-19). Their purpose to make the world a temple filled with the multiplied glory and goodness of God was curtailed when God's curse plunged all of creation into misery (Romans 8:20-23). Once disengaged from their mission and cut off from paradise (Genesis 3:24) — the place in which they could live freely as a people with purpose — humankind immediately began to distort creation's glory and goodness (see Genesis 4 for starters).

Tragically, we have inherited Adam and Eve's ruined relationships with God, people, and creation (Romans 5:12-21). We are now naturally inclined to believe that every*one* (God and people) and every*thing* (creation and all its resources) is here to serve *us*. Our fallen "community" of me-myself-and-I has adopted an almost exclusively me-first mission: making the world a temple of *our* praise by using every*one* and every*thing* for the exaltation and enhancement of *our* glory, not God's.

From Bad to Worse

Genesis 4-10 illustrates the intensified impact of sin as it passed from generation to generation and culture to culture. The me-first heart went viral. Genesis 11 tells a story that captures the essence of the brokenness Adam and Eve set into motion, because it is a story about a community with a mission.

The people who built the Tower of Babel sought the community and mission for which they were made but separate from dependence on the One who made them. They wanted to maintain relationship with heaven and with one another by building "a city and a tower" so that they could reach the heavens and not be "dispersed over the face of the whole earth." They wanted the *community* for which they were made, but on their own terms. They also held out hope that this project would help them make a name for themselves, an accomplishment that would leave a legacy. They wanted the *mission* for which they were made, but again, on their own terms.

Making Sense of My Story

Doesn't this shed some interesting light on my supposed glory days as a teenage Elvis impersonator? I was using the Elvis act to *be* some*one* special and *do* some*thing* special. I sinfully pursued the affection and the attention of my community, and my mission was to make a name for myself instead of living for the only name worthy of fame, Jesus Christ. I was designed to live life with a you-first heart, to relate and rule with God in his Kingdom, but the Elvis act was all about establishing my own me-first kingdom.

I look back now and laugh at the madness of my methods. I might be tempted to chalk it all up to youthful foolishness, but the truth is that as I grew older I simply found more subtle and sophisticated strategies to pursue the same twisted goals. In high school and college I tried drama club, getting good grades, student government, and the church youth choir as avenues for joining a community on mission. In my college and seminary days, local-church ministry and academic achievement were my means to be someone special and do something special. These days I'm tempted to depend on the behavior of my children, my religious reputation, praise for preaching and teaching and counseling skills, the number of hits on my blog, and a whole host of other ways in which I can relate to others and rule some small kingdom within my purview without depending on God. Even now I must fight against all the me-first reasons for writing this book.

Elvis is still in the building, still trying to do it his way. He just keeps changing costumes. Indeed, all of us are caught between the dignity of our design on the one hand and our depraved distortion of it on the other. We were created to live in community and on mission, but we pursue these things on our own terms, not God's.

What's your story? As you look back over your years, can you see the pattern I've described here? Are you aware that you were created to be cruciform, to enjoy right relationship with God, people, and all that God has made? Can you discern the ways in which you have pursued people and purpose apart from God? What are your Elvis stories?

Two

REDEEMED TO BE CRUCIFORM

I had never seen so much orange. The side streets of Knoxville had turned to raging rivers of color, sweeping my friend and me the two miles from our car, across campus, and finally to Neyland Stadium. It was my first University of Tennessee Volunteers home football game. I'll never forget cresting that last hill and standing in awe as a vast orange crowd flooded into the famous football fortress as if someone had pulled the stopper from a giant drain.

We were soon sucked through the main gates with volumes of other fans. Finally surfacing near our seats, we took in the vastness of one of the nation's largest open-air stadiums. The splendor of the Volunteer spirit filled that place to overflowing. The energy of antici-pation and the sights, sounds, and smells of "football time in Tennessee" almost took my breath away. A hundred choruses of "Rocky Top" gave way to a single, massive roar as our players ran out of their locker room, solemnly slapped the sign that says, "I will give my all for Tennessee today," and blasted onto the field.

As the game unfolded, there were moments of high drama when we seemed to be on the verge of defeat. I sat on the edge of my seat. I chewed my nails. Hope rose and sank in that orange sea like a fisherman's bobber. When our boys somehow pulled through and won the game, I leaped and yelled, pumping my fists in the air as if I had personally made the winning touchdown. All around me, complete strangers shared hugs and high-fives. We were all champions, each one a conqueror. We were the victorious Vol Nation.

What I experienced that day was glory. I was caught up in the glory of a community on mission, the glory of being someone special and doing something special. I felt that glory, saw and heard it magnified by a hundred thousand people, and even contributed to the glory with my own heart, head, and hands.

There is only one reason college football can do this. There is only one reason that we can be captivated and galvanized by any kind of collective activity, be it sports, the arts, politics, crafts, business ventures, online communities, social causes, or anything else. We were made to pursue and participate in the glory generated by a community on mission. We were made to be a *people* with a *purpose*. We really were born for glory.

There's nothing inherently wrong with enjoying Tennessee football—unless and until it turns into i-Volatry. And that's the tragic part. We so easily turn any community-on-mission into an idol. It happens the moment we define ourselves more by any community other than the community-on-mission for which God made us. When we look to some smaller community to save us from boredom and give us our primary sense of intimacy and effectiveness, we have joined with those who rallied around the Tower of Babel. We have begun to use that smaller community-on-mission to pursue a me-first search for glory.

Like the people who built the tower in Genesis 11, we all tend to live for the glory of *being* someone special and *doing* something special, but we try to do it on our own terms, apart from God. The reason it never really works and never really satisfies is that we were made for greater glory than that. Far greater glory.

Redemption

In sharp contrast to what took place a chapter before in Babel, Genesis 12 opens with God's stunning plan of redemption. As he did in the beginning, God chose one man from whom he would make a people for himself and his purposes. What makes this plan stunning is that God did not wipe the slate clean and start over. No, he did the unthinkable. Rather than throw all of us hell-bent sons and rebellious servants in a landfill, the holy and righteous Creator salvaged some to build the cruciform cathedral—the you-first, God-first community called the church—he had planned from the beginning. God's promise to Abraham in Genesis 12 lays out his plan:

Now the LORD said to Abram, "Go from your country and your kindred and your father's house to the land that I will show you. And I will make of you a great nation, and I will bless you and make your name great, so that you will be a blessing. I will bless those who bless you, and him who dishonors you I will curse, and in you all the families of the earth shall be blessed." (Genesis 12:1-3)

John Stott highlights the prominence of these promises: "It may be truly said without exaggeration that not only the rest of the Old Testament but the whole of the New Testament are an outworking of these promises of God."[3] These verses unveil God's blueprint for redeeming and rebuilding his cruciform cathedral. God plans to choose a people whom he will bless by bringing them into loving relationship with himself. He will then change these me-first idolaters into you-first image-bearers who, in blessed community with God and one another, will *be* someone special and *do* something special toward the fulfillment of God's mission to bless the world.

First, God planned to adopt and bless a people. When God promises Abraham, "I will bless you," he is repeating and restoring the blessing he originally gave his first son and servant, Adam, in Genesis 1:28. Abraham and his descendants would enjoy a special relationship with God based on nothing more than

God's gracious promise to lovingly choose them as people he made special and would faithfully use to do something special (Deuteronomy 7:6-8). The community that would come from Abraham, later called Israel, would be God's adopted son and servant (Genesis 35:10-11, Exodus 4:22-23, Hosea 1:10).

Second, God planned to assemble this people as his beloved community. God's promise to make Abraham's people "a great nation," blessing those who bless them and cursing those who dishonor them, undergirds his plan to build them into a privileged community whom God himself protects and for whom God provides. Later, under the ministry of Moses, God would give this people the Law, a more detailed blueprint for building a cross-shaped community functioning as his "kingdom of priests and a holy nation" (Exodus 19:6). In this Law, summarized by the Ten Commandments, God showed Israel what it would look like to live as a God-centered community of people who love God with all their head, heart, and hands (commandments one through four), and who love their neighbors as they love themselves (commandments five through ten) (see Exodus 20:1-17; Leviticus 19:18; Deuteronomy 5:1-21, 6:4-5). They were to be cross-shaped, a graciously chosen and blessed community of people in right *vertical* relationship with God and right *horizontal* relationship with one another in the place God had them. [4] God made them to be, and then caused them to be, a people special to him, to one another, and to the world.

<u>**Third, God planned to apprentice this people in his mission to bless the world.**</u> God redeemed his collective son Israel to serve with him as a kingdom of priests who would pick up where Adam and Eve had left off. They would do this by loving God and each other, and by preparing the place where God had put them. Preparing it as a dwelling place for God and people. Preparing it by guarding and keeping all creatures and creation for the glory of God and the good of others. God would therefore strengthen his servant Israel to do something special (Isaiah 41:8-10). Their mission was to bless their neighbors, the nations, and the next generation by pointing them to God's glory and goodness. Eventually, this would include inviting Gentiles to become part of God's community and mission (Genesis 12:3, Deuteronomy 26:18-19, Galatians 3:8).

Bad News

But as we read the Old Testament, it's clear this plan was never fully worked out. Even with great men like Moses and David leading them, God's sons and servants continued to be runaway rebels. Under King David's reign, God's blueprint for an adopted community apprenticed on his mission began to approach reality, but then it all fell apart again. Throughout Israel's history, sin repeatedly divided God's community and distracted them from his mission. Any contractor knows that a structure is only as strong as its materials, and something had to be done about these faulty building blocks, these sinners God had been using to build his sanctuary. But God had a plan to deal with sin. And though there had always been provisions made for sin through the sacrifices of atonement God had granted, these were only a shadow of God's ultimate plan to make strong bricks out of sinful people (Hebrews 10:1-18).

We pick up the story with God's people in exile. Once again, just as in Eden, they were kicked out of God's place and outside of his blessing because they refused to live under his rule.⁵ Not only had they profaned God's name in their own land, they continued to do so even while being punished in exile (Ezekiel 36:16-21). But God intended to vindicate his good name. Had I been the architect, I would have trashed the building blocks and started from scratch with better ones, but God didn't do that. He would build a cathedral that would vindicate his name, but he would use the very people who had shamed his name. And so God's people began to hear through his prophets about a New Covenant, a new set of promises that would deal with sin and complete the blueprint for God's holy dwelling place in our hearts (Jeremiah 31:31-34). God knew he must do something about the me-first hearts of his hell-bent sons and rebellious servants, so through the prophet Ezekiel he unpacked the New Covenant promises to God's people: a new purity, a new passion, a new power, and a new partnership.

A New Purity. "I will sprinkle clean water on you,

and you shall be clean from all your uncleannesses, and from all your idols I will cleanse you" (Ezekiel 36:25). Purification must come first. In order to be God's true sons and servants, the people must be unilaterally, voluntarily, and completely forgiven by God for rejecting his community, rebelling against his mission, and embracing idolatry. Idolatry is the reliance upon or trust in anyone or anything besides the Living God for community and mission (Jeremiah 2:11-13, Exodus 32:7-8). God had a plan to forgive and thus purify the people from their idolatry.

A New Passion. "And I will give you a new heart, and a new spirit I will put within you. And I will remove the heart of stone from your flesh and give you a heart of flesh" (Ezekiel 36:26). What do you do with building blocks whose hearts are desperately wicked, diamond-hard, and determined to do evil (Genesis 6:5, Jeremiah 17:9, Zechariah 7:12)? God's plan was literally to transform his people, turning their passionately me-first hearts into hearts that looked to him and others and said, *You first.*

A New Power. "And I will put my Spirit within you, and cause you to walk in my statutes and be careful to obey my rules" (Ezekiel 36:27). It was painfully apparent that God's people had no power to keep his royal law, so God promised the gift of his Spirit to empower them to live the cruciform life of vertical love for God and horizontal love for people. His Spirit will be the power supply for a you-first heart.

A New Partnership. "You shall dwell in the land that I gave to your fathers, and you shall be my people, and I will be your God" (Ezekiel 36:28). This is one of the sweetest and most often repeated promises in the Bible. It's the assurance that the disobedience of God's people will not dissuade him from partnering with them as a holy community on his holy mission.

God would claim, clean, and craft for himself a people who would live the cruciform life of loving God and others as it is required in his Law. He would forgive them for living a me-first life and give them a new heart and the power of his Spirit to live the you-first life they were made to live. Now that's good news!

Good News

Good news, indeed. *Gospel* means "good news." The promised plan of God to create a cruciform community with a new purity, passion, power, and partnership would come through the life, death, and resurrected life of his Son and Servant, Jesus Christ. So we fast-forward to the end of the New Testament Gospels where Jesus, when he lifted the cup of wine at the Last Supper, said, "This cup is the New Covenant in my blood, which is poured out for many for the forgiveness of sins" (see Matthew 26:28, Mark 14:24, Luke 22:20, 1 Corinthians 11:25). With this statement, backed up by his life, ministry, crucifixion, and resurrection, Jesus became "the mediator of a new covenant," the promised righteous Servant, the ultimate priest who offers himself as the sacrifice for the guilt of his people to "make many to be accounted righteous" (Hebrews 9:15, Isaiah 52:13-53:12).

Jesus lived the cruciform life of loving God and others, the life that God's first son and servant (Adam), and God's adopted sons and servants (Israel) had failed to live. He died by a crucifixion that all of us deserve: "he was wounded for our transgressions; he was crushed for our iniquities" (Isaiah 53:5). Then God raised him from the dead to prove that, by his cross, Jesus had triumphed over God's adversary, the devil (Genesis 3:15, Acts 2:24, Colossians 2:15). It is by faith in Jesus as the perfectly obedient son and the perfect offering for sin in our place that we are finally and completely restored, having been reconciled to and made right with God (2 Corinthians 5:17-21, Romans 3:21-26). In Christ, both Jews and Gentiles "are being built together into a dwelling place for God by the Spirit" (Ephesians 2:22). Through the gospel we enter the reality of the promise that our corrupt, me-first life will be forgiven and progressively replaced with a cross-shaped, you-first life of glory by the power of the Spirit (2 Corinthians 3:18). Through Jesus we are shaped *by* the cross into the shape *of* the cross.

If we discarded stones are connected by faith to Jesus, the Cornerstone, as he is offered in the gospel, then the Architect has adopted us as sons and apprenticed us as servants who work to make all of creation the temple or sanctuary of God, the place where God's glory is seen and sensed by our neighbors, the nations, and the next generation. "Our task as the covenant community, the church," writes G. K. Beale, "is to be God's temple, so filled with his glorious presence that we expand and fill the earth with that presence until God finally accomplishes the goal completely at the end of time!" [6]

Only the gospel can build this cruciform cathedral. The gospel preached to Abraham broke ground for the formation of God's redeemed community-on-mission (Galatians 3:8-9). The gospel that Jesus preached and paid for with his blood gathered an initial community of disciples to continue his mission in the power of the Spirit (Luke 4:43, 24:50-53; Acts 1:6-14). The gospel is the message of the cross by which the Apostles established God's spiritual house (Acts 2:36-47). Today, by the proclamation of the gospel *to* God's people and *by* God's people, this cruciform community is continuing to be built up for maturity and ministry (1 Corinthians 15:1-11, Colossians 1:3-6, 1 Peter 2:4-10). One day soon the project will be complete and we will hear "a loud voice from the throne saying, 'Behold, the dwelling place of God is with man. He will dwell with them, and they will be his people, and God himself will be with them as their God'" (Revelation 21:3). And when the gospel is said and done the glory of God will fill creation "as the waters cover the sea" (Numbers 14:21, Psalm 72:19, Habakkuk 2:14, Isaiah 11:9).

That's a glory story worth getting out of bed in the morning to pursue, saying, "By God's transforming power, I will give my all for Jesus Christ today." It's game time. Let's hit the field!

Three
THE ELEMENTS OF BEING CRUCIFORM

The Gospel accounts of Jesus' life, along with the prescription for the Christian life found in the rest of the New Testament, have convinced me there are two major roles in which disciples progressively become like their Master (Luke 6:40). As we each become more and more conformed to the image of Christ, we increasingly live as a *son* and love as a *servant*. The rest of this book is built on this idea of disciples being both sons and servants.

Through salvation, life for a Christian is redefined. From the moment we are adopted into God's family, we hold these dual roles of son and servant. I want to help you better understand the implications of having these two roles, which are distinct, yet permanently joined. Along the way, I want to change the way you look at the image of the cross.

It is no coincidence that the cross is the dominant,

universal image of the Christian faith. First and foremost, the cross represents that central moment in human history when Christ paid for the sins of mankind, thus satisfying the righteous wrath of God the Father. But that simple image also symbolizes a more elaborate theology, one that has spoken to countless believers throughout history who have not had the benefit of either owning a Bible or knowing how to read. Part of the purpose of this book is to help recapture the simple and solidly biblical power of

- the vertical axis of the cross representing love for God
- the horizontal axis of the cross representing love for others
- the unity of the cross representing the inseparability of those two activities for the believer.

What does it mean to be a cruciform disciple? The rest of this book seeks to answer that question. The rest of this chapter introduces the elements of the answer.

Beloved Sons and Blessed Servants

First, a cruciform disciple to some degree resembles Jesus the Son, who lived in complete awareness of and dependence upon his relationship to God as the Father's beloved (Matthew 3:17, 17:5; Mark 1:11, 9:7; 2 Peter 1:17). By wholly believing the message of the cross, we too become beloved sons of God (John 1:12, Romans 8:14-17, Galatians 4:4-7). The more we become like Jesus, the Beloved Son, the more we will fill up by faith on the love of the Father through the gospel as his beloved sons.

Ladies—you may want to review Galatians 3:26-29, where both men and women are said to be "sons of God." An adopted son in Paul's day was a full heir while adopted daughters were not. But in Christ, both men and women are full heirs and therefore both are called "sons."[7]

Second, a cruciform disciple to some degree resembles Jesus the Servant, who lived in the complete awareness and practice of his role as a blessed servant to God, people, and all of creation (Mark 10:43-45). Jesus' confidence and contentment in his relationship with the Father enabled him to lay aside his rights, pick up the towel and basin, and take the form of a servant by emptying himself for the sake of others (John 13:3-5, Philippians 2:5-11). As we fill up by faith on the love of the Father as it is offered in the good news about Jesus and poured out by the Spirit, we overflow with love back to God and out to others, using the resources he has provided in the place he has put us. Our lives will take the form of a cross-shaped servant.

The Servant: Seeker, Shepherd, Sower, Steward

Let me introduce a simple illustration of how we are sons and servants:

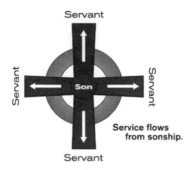

Now let's add another layer. The role of servant takes on more specific forms as the disciple relates to God, to other believers, to unbelieving neighbors, and to all that God has made.

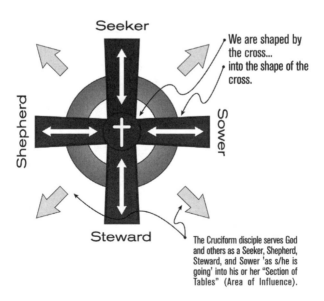

In relationship to God, the servant is a Seeker: one who exalts God by seeking first the Lord, his kingdom, and his righteousness (Matthew 6:33; Colossians 3:1-4; Hebrews 11:6, 11:8-16, 13:14). Like Jesus, we seek to imitate the Father's every word and work, longing to think like him, love like him, and act like him (John 5:19, 5:30, 7:16, 8:28, 13:34, 14:10, 14:24, 15:9). Like Jesus, in regular times of solitude and prayer, we share the psalmists' desire to "seek the Lord and his strength; seek his presence continually" as we serve the people in our circles of influence (Psalm 105:4; Luke 5:16, 11:1-13).

In relationship to other disciples, the servant is a Shepherd: one who *encourages* brothers and sisters in Christ, who loves and labors with them for the sake of the kingdom (Acts 2:42-47, 4:32; Romans 1:11-12; Ephesians 5:18-21; Colossians 3:12-16; 2 Timothy 2:22; Hebrews 3:12-13, 10:19-25). This is obviously not to say that every believer plays the specific role of pastor or elder. But it is to say that in imitation of Jesus we are to know some of his sheep by name, and in real ways we are to care for them, protect them, feed them, and urge them to follow his voice and his lead (John 10:1-4). As the Lamb of God sacrificially served his fellow lambs, we too must lay down our lives to help our brothers and sisters satisfy their souls with the abundant life of knowing him and the Father who sent him (John 1:29, 10:10-11, 13:34-35, 17:2-3).

Like our Good Shepherd, we also know the Father has "other sheep who are not of this fold." These we must call to him, enfolding them into our community as "one flock" under "one shepherd" (John 10:16). This leads to our next category.

In relationship to others who are not disciples, the servant is a Sower: one who *engages* neighbors, the nations, and the next generation with the love of Christ by sowing the good news of God's kingdom into his or her spheres of influence through works of service and words of witness (Isaiah 58:10-12; Psalm 80, Matthew 13:1-43, 25:31-46, 28:18-20; Mark 4:26-32; John 4:31-38; Romans 1:13-17; 2 Corinthians 9:6-15; Acts 1:8; Galatians 5:6b, 6:8-10; James 1:27, 3:18). We must be like Jesus who, "when he saw the crowds, he had compassion for them, because they were harassed and helpless, like sheep without a shepherd" (Matthew 9:36). Jesus urges us as his disciples to see our circles of influence as a ready harvest; he asks us to pray for God to send laborers into the harvest; he then sends us into the harvest as the answer to our prayers and his (Matthew 9:37-38, 10:5-6; John 17:21-23).

In relationship to all that God has made, the servant is a Steward: one who is continually *equipped* by God's Word to use the resources (body, time, talents/gifts, money, head/heart/hands, words, work, creation) that God has given us for the work and witness of the kingdom (Matthew 24:45-51; Romans 12:1-2; 1 Corinthians 10:31; Colossians 3:17, 23-24; 1 Peter 4:10-11). Like Jesus, we know that we are here not to do our own will but "to do the will of the one who sent [us] and to accomplish his work," thus glorifying the Father in our circles of influence (John 4:34, 5:30, 6:38, 17:4).

Big Cross, Little Cross

In the diagrams on page 38, the *big cross* represents both the cross-shaped life of Jesus and your cross-shaped life as you are being conformed to his image. The *little cross* in the center (actually not little at all) represents the gospel that has the power to transform you into one who takes up your cross to live and love like Jesus. This is my way of illustrating a truth that Jerry Bridges makes clear:

> The most important message we need to hear as believers is the gospel. It is not the only message; we do need to hear the requirements of discipleship. But the gospel is the most important, because it alone provides both the proper motive and the only enduring motivation to respond to our Lord's call to discipleship. [8]

The Two-Way Arrows

You'll notice that the diagram has two-way arrows that connect the little cross and the big cross, the inner role of Son with the outer role of Servant. These arrows illustrate the interplay between the moral Law of God and the gospel. [9]

The outward-facing arrows indicate the love of Christ compelling us to love and live with you-first hearts (2 Corinthians 5:14-15, Titus 2:11-14). As the gospel (through which we understand ourselves to be beloved sons) transforms us, our lives conform to the moral Law. This Law prescribes the cruciform life of *vertical* love for God and *horizontal* love for others (Matthew 22:36-40). The role of Servant and its four expressions (Seeker, Shepherd, Sower, Steward) represent the Law being practiced in our relationships with God, people, and creation as evidence that we truly have come to know God and his love through the gospel (1 John 2:3, 2:15-17, 3:1-10, 4:7-21). As we *embrace the gospel* by faith, we *express the Law* by loving God and others (Galatians 5:6). "We love because he first loved us" (1 John 4:19).

The inward-facing arrows indicate our continuing need to come back to the cross for fresh grace as we repent of our failure to love God and others (Luke 7:36-50, 18:9-14; Galatians 3:1-5, 5:6; Colossians 2:6-7; 1 Corinthians 15:1-2; 1 Timothy 1:15-16; 1 John 2:1-2). As we pursue by faith a life of Spirit-empowered obedience to God's Law, we will come to find all the ways we still fall short of the Law (Romans 7:22-8:1).

By faith we will *seek* God, only to find that we don't seek him well or worthily, so we will return to the cross with this new insight into our remaining sin (Revelation 2:4-5).

By faith we will *shepherd* our fellow brothers and sisters in Christ, only to find out how selfish we still are and how hard it is to forgive. We will again understand our need to repent and run to Jesus to embrace the grace given us so we can give it to our fellow servants (Matthew 6:12, 18:21-35).

By faith we will *sow* in our areas of influence, only to discover how little we love our unbelieving neighbors, how little we care about the nations, and how often we ignore the next generation. We'll be driven back to the cross for fresh grace to love others like Jesus does (Philippians 2:1-18).

By faith we will *steward* the resources God has given us, only to be convicted afresh by how we use them for our sake, not his, and we will run like the wasteful, prodigal son back to our forgiving Father and ask to be clothed with Jesus again (Luke 15:11-24, 1 John 2:15-17).

We must remember, however, that it is not merely our *failure* to be seekers, shepherds, stewards, and sowers that should drive us back to the cross. Our *success* in these roles must drive us to Christ as well. George Whitefield, one of the evangelists God used to spark the Great Awakening, explained that one must not only repent of *failure* to obey God's Law, but

> [Y]ou must be brought to see that God may damn you for the best prayer you ever put up . . . that all your duties . . . are so far from recommending you to God. . . . you must not only be made sick of your original and actual sin, but you must be made sick of your righteousness, of all your duties and performances. [10]

At times, you will notice that you're doing quite well as a Seeker: you enjoy consistent times of prayer and maintain a kingdom perspective in your everyday affairs. Just then pride rushes in, "I *am* doing well, aren't

I? Well, good for me!" Or perhaps you'll see that you steward your time, money, body, or whatever, better than the other folks in your small group, and a sinister smugness begins to rear its ugly head. Perhaps one day you'll believe that since you shared the gospel with that guy on the plane, God owes you a break from suffering or a positive answer to a selfish prayer. These are ways in which our *successes* as servants quickly turn to self-righteousness. Anytime I begin to depend on my own performance as a Seeker, Shepherd, Steward, or Sower for right standing with God and others, I need to run back to the cross and repent of my self-righteousness.

So whether repenting of our Law-breaking or our Law-keeping, we each return often to the cross. From there, God propels us back into the world as his as beloved sons and blessed servants (2 Corinthians 5:14-15). That's the nature of God's grace. When you receive it by faith, it always pushes you back out into a life of loving God and others (Titus 2:11-14).

The Circle

The circle that connects the arms of our Celtic cross represents the connectedness of the vertical life of love for God and the horizontal life of loving others. "We love because he first loved us," wrote the Apostle John. "If anyone says, 'I love God,' and hates his brother, he is a liar; for he who does not love his brother whom he has seen cannot love God whom he has not seen. And this commandment we have from him: whoever loves God must also love his brother" (1 John 4:19-21). I cannot respond any better than G. W. Barker did in his commentary on this letter: "John makes clear that obedience expresses itself in a single command. Love for God and love of neighbor are inseparable. The one is not possible apart from the other."[11]

The circle also conveys another connectedness: it reminds us the roles of Seeker, Shepherd, Steward, and Sower are not neatly compartmentalized. In any given time or place we will be fulfilling one or more of these roles. These are not hats you change, announcing, "Excuse me, I'm going to be a Sower now." They merely help us understand the various expressions by which we serve God, people, and creation.

The As-You-Are-Going Arrows

These are the four arrows that move away from the corners of the Celtic cross. We'll learn more about these in Chapter Five, but for now these represent the as-you-are-goings of your daily life. In the original language of Matthew 28:19, Jesus did not actually say "*Go* into all the world" but "*As you are going* into all the world. . . ." The only command in that verse is to "make disciples of all nations"; the "going" part is assumed.

So we move into our various roles, responsibilities, and relationships with this in mind: as I go in and out of my areas of influence, all my activities as a son and a servant simply represent my participation in the fulfillment of God's promise to Abraham, that through us

(Abraham's spiritual offspring) God would bless all the nations of the earth (Genesis 12:2-3).

Thus, as our Father's adopted children and apprentices, we are being restored to our original purpose:

- to live in right relationship with God and people
- as we participate in his plan to reconcile all that he has made to himself through the cross
- for the glory of God and the good of neighbors, nations, and the next generation
- in the places he has put us (Colossians 1:19-23, Ephesians 1:22-23).

The Cruciform Community

The cross-shaped diagram we have been examining represents the cruciform cathedral that Jesus is building by bringing together his cruciform disciples, his "living stones," into localized cruciform communities we call churches (Matthew 16:18, Ephesians 2:19-22, 1 Peter 2:4-10):

> The church is now the place on earth where God primarily dwells and makes himself known. This temple is not made with human hands but exists in the corporate life of those who have been transformed through faith in Christ. The presence and work of God in worship, the ministry of the Word, service to others, discipline, baptism, the Lord's Supper, and gospel proclamation are now the primary source of the presence and glory of God in the world. [12]

As the diagram below illustrates, a cruciform community is a devoted family of cross-shaped disciples who live as God's community-on-mission to share and show the gospel to the world.

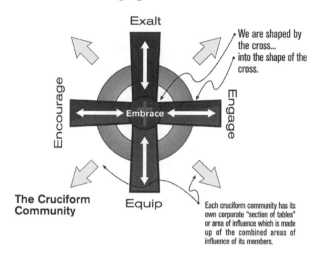

As the diagram suggests, the members of such communities are corporately committed to *being* cruciform disciples and *making* cruciform disciples in the following ways.

Embrace. We fill up on God's love as we embrace the gospel of the kingdom (Acts 2:41).

Exalt and Equip. We overflow with love so that, as seekers in worship (Acts 2:42b, 46, 47a) we exalt God, and as stewards in instruction (Acts 2:42a) we equip disciples.

Encourage and Engage. We overflow with love so that, by shepherding one another in fellowship (Acts 2:44-45) we encourage disciples, and by sowing expressions of service and witness (Acts 2:43) we engage our world with the love of Christ. [13]

That is our introduction to the cross diagram—an aid to help us think about, visualize, and remember how God is at work in us to glorify himself and do good to men and women. I pray that as we build from this blueprint in the coming chapters it will be as helpful for you as it has been for me, enabling all of us to become better established in Christ by the gospel, "being built together into a dwelling place for God by the Spirit" (Ephesians 2:22).

Four
THE CRUCIFORM LIFE IN ACTION

One October as the fall colors peaked in the Blue Ridge Mountains, I participated in a prayer retreat with four other local pastors. Buddy, our retreat leader, had taken us on these before. Typically we would go to a wonderfully quiet place to spend thirty-six silent hours with God, coming together only for meals, which we also shared in silence. These retreats were precious opportunities to fast from speaking and to feast on the Savior. [14]

This time, Buddy had arranged for us to stay at a slice-of-heaven Young Life camp called Windy Gap. When I first heard the news, I assumed that because school was in session the place would be empty. That sounded perfect. I was in a season of weariness, and my heart rose as I imagined the blissful silence and isolation awaiting us.

But Buddy, and God, had other plans. In fact, Buddy had warned us that this retreat might look a little different. He was right about that. On the way to the camp we learned there would be 120 Young Life staff there, and Buddy had signed up the five of us to be their silent kitchen crew.

"Now, this might be good news to some of you guys," Buddy said, "because I know you feel more comfortable serving people than sitting in silence and solitude. But I want you to use these times of service as an added opportunity to commune with Christ. So, we'll just serve in silence, and when we're not working or sharing meals, we'll seek solitude." This was not a welcome surprise for me. I could not relate to what Buddy was saying about being more comfortable serving than sitting. I had come on this retreat to get *away* from serving people. I was ready to settle into silence, solitude, and *not* serving.

But that wasn't my only concern. Qualms and questions flooded into my mind because I had never done anything quite like this before: *Will I know what to do? Will I do a good job? What about this genetic tremor in my hands? Will I drop something? What about my deaf left ear? Will I misunderstand something said to me, or not hear it at all? What will people think of me?*

Perhaps worst of all, I realized I would be without words, my best means of self-defense. No explanatory words to disclose my physical limitations. No humorous or sarcastic words to deflect attention away from my poor performance or to defend or excuse my mistakes. It came down to this: any hope of dressing up my me-first heart with you-first-sounding words had been smashed like a dropped plate.

As I suspected, serving as kitchen crew was messy, physically draining, time-consuming, and humbling. I was left with nothing to depend on...except Jesus. And of course, that was the point. My Lord had called me to be with him in that place at that time, and he had arranged the circumstances so I had no choice but to look to him for the direction, strength, and motivation I needed to serve on his terms.

When the retreat was over I knew two things to be true: during those few mute hours in the kitchen I had presented a badly flawed model *of* Christlike servanthood, but I had also learned a great deal *about* Christlike servanthood. I had learned, in a completely new way and at a completely new level, that the cruciform life in action is about serving—serving God and serving others while depending on his Son.

Jesus, the Son and Servant

Jesus has not called us to live a life that he has not lived himself. As our trailblazer, he first embraced the love and leadership of his Father by faith, and he then expressed that faith in loving servanthood. His entire earthly ministry had a single purpose: to pour himself out for the sake of seeing people and creation reconciled to a right relationship with God and one another (Hebrews 12:2, Philippians 2:5-11, Colossians 1:19-20). A quick scan through the Gospels reveals two crucial roles by which Jesus identified himself and out of which he lived—the roles of son and servant, introduced in the previous chapter.

Jesus lived as the Father's *Son.* This means Jesus lived in constant awareness of and dependence upon his relationship to God as his Father's *beloved.* Recall that the two most important and intense phases of Jesus' life on earth were preceded by strikingly similar experiences. Jesus' baptism inaugurated his public ministry (Matthew 3:17, Mark 1:10, Luke 3:22), and his transfiguration began the transition to his Passion Week ministry (Matthew 17:5, Mark 9:7, Luke 9:35, 2 Peter 1:17). Following both of those events, Jesus heard these words from his Father: "This is my beloved Son, with whom I am well pleased."

We know from the Apostle John's testimony that Jesus frequently mentioned that he was God's Son (John 5:17-18, 10:32-38, and more) and that he was fully aware of and dependent upon his Father's love for him (John 3:35, 5:20, 10:17, 15:9-10, 17:23-26). Paul's reference to Jesus as "the Beloved" and the "Beloved Son" suggests that this emphasis on the Son's close relationship with his Father was passed down through the Apostles' teaching (Ephesians 1:6; Colossians 1:13; 2 Peter 1:17-18; 1 John 1:1-3, 2:22-24, 4:10-15; 2 John 3).

Jesus also lived as the Father's *Servant.* This means Jesus lived in constant, obedient awareness of his relationship to God as the Father's *blessed servant.*

Jesus made it clear that he "came not to be served but to serve" (Matthew 20:28, Mark 10:45). He gave the disciples a memorable picture of what that service meant when he washed their feet at the Last Supper (a task left to the lowliest of servants) and, the *very next day*, he "made himself nothing, taking the form of a servant" and became "obedient to the point of death, even death on a cross" (John 13:1-17, Philippians 2:7-8).

Perhaps only after the ascension and the outpouring of the Spirit at Pentecost did the Apostles truly understand what their Master had meant when he said, "I am among you as one who serves" (Luke 22:27). After Pentecost, the Apostles and earliest followers of Jesus identified him as God's "holy servant" both in their preaching and their prayers (Acts 3:13, 3:26, 4:27-30). Both Jesus and his followers believed that he was the "suffering servant" whom Isaiah prophesied would one day pour out his life for the sake of God's people (Isaiah 52:13-53:12, Luke 22:37, Acts 8:32-35).

He Has Given Us an Example

Jesus' washing of the disciples' feet is the perfect picture of the cruciform life, a life of loving service that flows from a loved son. Jesus knew that he forever belonged to the Father and would forever be with and beside the Father (John 13:3). John makes it clear that from his position and power as Son, Jesus fulfilled his purpose as Servant, obeying his Father by taking up his cross with a you-first heart that says, "not my will, but yours, be done" (Luke 22:42). Jesus the Son and Suffering Servant poured out his blood from the basin of his perfect life. He took the towel of his flesh and wiped away our sins. The life, death, and resurrected life of Jesus is an example of the cruciform life in action, a life that says to God and others, "I am among you as one who serves" (Luke 22:27). Jesus has now handed his cross-shaped ministry of reconciliation over to us, saying "you also should do just as I have done to you" (2 Corinthians 5:17-21, John 13:15).

Embraced as Sons, Empowered and Employed as Servants

Jesus calls us to serve like him but, as we've discovered, his service has ever flowed from his Sonship. Our service must also flow from sonship, for unless and until we are sons we can't serve, won't serve, and don't want to serve. Without divine sonship, we are like the two lost sons in Luke 15:11-32. That is, we have rejected the fellowship freely offered to us by the Father and instead embraced either pleasure (trying to escape God's righteousness) or performance (trying to earn it). We are ruled by "the passions of our flesh" rather than the passions of our Father (Ephesians 2:1-3). We cannot live the cross-shaped life of lovingly serving God and others until we have been forgiven and formed by the cross of Christ.

The difference between Jesus' Sonship and ours is that he has always been God's Son by the nature of his being, while we become sons by adoption when we embrace the gospel by faith (John 1:12-13, 3:1-15; Galatians 4:4-6). When through the gospel we have become sons, then through the gospel we can become servants. There are at least three ways in which sonship empowers servanthood.

- As sons of the Father, we have been *forgiven* (1 Peter 1:14-21). The debt of guilt we carried before God was paid for us at the cross. God has shown us mercy; therefore, we can share this mercy with others in the places God puts us (Matthew 18:21-35).

- As Jesus' *friends and family* we have been invited to participate in fulfilling the plans of his kingdom (John 15:12-17, Hebrews 2:10-11, Luke 12:32), which is a kingdom of service.

- Finally, we are being *formed* into Christ-like servants ever so surely by the Spirit who now lives in us (2 Corinthians 3:18).

To elaborate on that last point, the very Spirit by whom we cry "Abba, Father" is the One whose name means "helper" or "one who comes alongside" (Romans 8:14-17, John 14:15-17). He knows how to make sons into servants who come alongside others with a you-first heart. This is the Spirit who gives us various gifts in order that we may serve others with holy hospitality (1 Corinthians 12:4-11, 1 Peter 4:7-11). This is the Spirit who continues to bear witness to us about Jesus and empowers us to bear witness about Christ to others (John 15:26-27, Acts 1:8). And this is the Spirit who

provided the blood of Christ that cleanses our con-
sciences from dead works and causes us to walk in the
good works of love for God and others (Ezekiel 36:22-28,
Hebrews 9:14, Titus 3:4-8).

In sum, we are the forgiven friends and family
of Jesus, whose Spirit is forming us to be cruciform
servants who love like our crucified Servant.

Expressing the Law by Embracing the Gospel

In Chapter Three, I explained that living as a servant by
loving God and others is an expression of the Law of
God, and that obeying the Law flows from embracing
the gospel as a son. The Law of God is something
commanded that we must *do*. The gospel is something
completed for us that Christ has *done.* As these two
realities come together, something unique in the human
experience takes place: by virtue of being sons—rooted
and grounded by faith in the love given us through
the *completed actions* of Christ's life, death, and resurrection (Ephesians 3:17-19)—we become able to obey the
Law's *commands* to love God and others as a servant.

Of course, as every Christian has experienced,
only the Son of God, the Suffering Servant, can obey
God's Law fully. For us to be Law-keepers, we must
be united by faith to God's Son (Romans 8:3-4), so that
his perfect Law-keeping is counted as ours. We must
not fall into the Galatian trap of getting the Law cart
before the gospel horse (Galatians 3:1-5). We are not

transformed into cruciform servants by buckling down in our own fleshly power to try harder at serving God and others. On the contrary, we pursue a life of serving God and others by faith as we hear, believe, and act on the message of the cross. This message tells us that we can count ourselves as actual sons of God, dead to our sinful me-first hearts and alive to God as servants with a you-first heart and an at-your-service life (Romans 6:5-14).

Served by the King for Kingdom Service

Serving at Windy Gap served me well. That first day of waiting tables was a struggle for my me-first heart. I selfishly wanted to be served by enjoying time alone with Jesus in restful retreat, but there I was serving other servants of Jesus who had come away for retreat themselves. The first afternoon I finally had a couple of hours alone with God, listening for his voice in his Word, but I did not sense he was saying anything to me in particular. I wrote in my journal, "Perhaps he will have something to say to me tonight at communion."

Later that evening I sat alone with my sinful, sulking, sick-of-serving heart in the corner of the upstairs room where we were celebrating the Lord's Supper. The room was dark except for the flickering light of candles on a long, low table that also supported a cross, the bread, and the cup. I got up and moved toward the table, and in a moment everything changed.

Later I recorded the experience in my journal: "As soon as I sat down and looked at the table, tears began to roll down my cheeks, and I had this overwhelming sense that the Father was saying to me, *See Jimmy, I love you! You are my son, my beloved. I am well-pleased with you because of Jesus. This cup is the New Covenant sealed for you by the blood of My Son. Your sins are forgiven—you are clean! You have a new heart that loves Me and wants to obey Me! Haven't you noticed? You have My Spirit living in you. Think about that! I love you, son. I delight in you. You bring Me joy.*"

When the bread and juice came around to me, there were more tears as I tasted the sweetness of my King's love for me. I realized then that I had been acting like Peter as he refused Jesus' offer to wash his feet. I wanted to serve God on my own terms and in my own strength, rejecting the idea that I needed something from God before I would truly be equipped to serve others. That night, God reminded me that before I can obediently *serve* my King I must be served the gospel *by* my King. So once again, he served me the gospel, so that I could become a gospel servant to him and others.

Five
SERVANTS OF GOD

The Shape of the Cross

No doubt about it, kitchen crew is hot and hard work. At Windy Gap the five of us arrived an hour before mealtime to help the cook staff prepare the food. When the guests filed in we each had a section of four or five tables assigned to us. Afterward we cleaned up and prepared the tables for the next meal. This all painted a vivid picture for me of what it means to be God's servant and to live among the people in my world as a son who comes not to be served, but to serve. [15]

Equipped to Serve

God's goal is to build his cathedral with people who live and love like Jesus, as sons who serve. In Ephesians 4, when Paul was laying out his God-given plan for building up the people of God into a cruciform cathedral, he gave instructions as to how the individual building blocks, the saints, were to be prepared for their place in the building. Pastors and church leaders, Paul explained, were to "equip the saints for the work of ministry, for building up the body of Christ," resulting in a unity and maturity that finds its final expression in love (Ephesians 4:11-16).

The Greek word translated "ministry" here is related to the word *diakonos*, a servant who waited tables at meals (see Luke 10:40, 12:37, 17:8, 22:27; John 12:2). At banquets and dinners the *diakonos* was assigned a certain number of tables over which he or she presided as one who watched, waited for, and willingly served the people who reclined and dined there. This was similar to how restaurants today assign servers to care for the guests at a particular section of tables. This is the kind of service Jesus referred to when he said, "For who is the greater, one who reclines at table or one who serves? Is it not the one who reclines at table? But I am among you as the one who serves" (Luke 22:27). Jesus was the chief *diakonos*.

Each follower of Jesus has been assigned a "section" of "tables," each of which is full of people who are in need of the ministry (*diakonian*, "service") of reconciliation to God (2 Corinthians 5:17-21). Some of these people need salvation, others need sanctification, but all need the God who comes to us in the gospel of grace. We who have been "served" reconciliation can now "serve" reconciliation to others on behalf of Christ (2 Corinthians 5:20). Paul called our section of tables our "area of influence"—the boundaries in which and the limits to which God has called us to multiply the glory of his community-on-mission through gospel works and witness (2 Corinthians 10:13-18).[16] The individual tables in our section are the circles of influence in which we live, the various as-you-are-goings we mentioned in Chapter Three such as home, work, neighborhood, school, stores, restaurants, the gym, extended family, clubs, teams, associations, church, etc. The work of ministry to which each of us is called is "to serve, not to be served," to live among those in our section of tables "as one who serves."

Another stick-man drawing may help you visualize this:

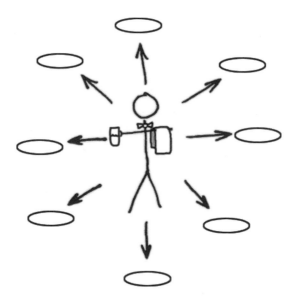

This drawing represents you, the servant. The arrows show that you have a God-and-others-oriented at-your-service heart, and the circles at the end of the arrows are the various "tables" or areas of influence to which God has assigned you as his servant.

Now, take a moment to label each table with a word that will signify the various circles of influence in which you've been placed and to which you go on at least a weekly basis. You may want to start at the top table and label it "home." Then continue to label the other tables: neighborhood, work/school, church, etc. Then, around each table write the names of at least three people whom you regularly see and interact with in that circle of influence. Once you've done that, you can see the people to whom God has called you to be a servant, just as Christ has served you. These are the people among whom you are to make disciples as-you-are-going (Matthew 28:18-20).

It's not a mystery who you are called to serve. Nor is it probably much of a mystery what each person needs. The unsaved need Christ, so we serve them to demonstrate God's sacrificial love. The saved need to grow closer to Christ, so we exhort and encourage them in the faith. (For a more detailed exercise in seeing and serving the people in your section of tables, download the Cruciform Life Tool Kit at www. cruciformlife.org.)

Watching, Waiting, Willing, Welcome

Once you've mapped out your section of tables, you'll probably find yourself in the same position I was in at the Windy Gap dining hall. *I've been assigned my section of tables, and I see the people there, but now what?* Allow me to suggest three activities and one attitude that you can begin to develop as you are going into your areas of influence on a daily or weekly basis.

Watching. Like a seasoned server in a fine restaurant, learn to look out for the needs of the people around you. Carefully and prayerfully consider the physical and spiritual needs of the people whom God brings across your path each day.

Our friend Sara excels at watching for the needs of others. Because of her our church plant had the opportunity to provide meals and prayers for a local family. Sara learned that in a single week, a neighborhood man had lost his job and his wife had major surgery. Their daughter was friends with Sara's daughter, and the family was new to town, with no family or friends to care for them. Seeing their lives in obvious turmoil, Sara began to serve these neighbors more intentionally. As she took care of the kids and brought the daughter to our worship gatherings, she was sowing gospel good works in this family's life. In a sense she was also shepherding the rest of us in the church plant by encouraging us to pray for the family. Eventually we had the opportunity to bless them with a cash gift for food and gas when they moved out of state.

Sara began this ministry by discerning her neighbors' needs and feeling compassion toward them. She began by simply paying attention to them like a good servant. The general manager of the Oceana restaurant in New York City said a good server must similarly learn to "read guests" at the tables:

> I think being in your station, watching the table, watching people eat, making eye contact to see what the body language is, is how you accurately read a guest. . . . You have to be watching. You have to be paying attention. You have to be looking. You have to be reading the table. [17]

Sara knows how to watch "tables" and read "guests." This family in Sara's area of influence were not believers, and as far as I know still aren't, but because Sara served them, they got a window seat with a view of the cross-shaped glory of God on display in his church.

Waiting. Waiting tables requires the server to anticipate that needs will arise, make himself *available* to meet them, and move into action to serve when the time is right. For the serving saint this requires a readiness that only seeking the Lord in prayer can provide.

In Chapter One we learned that every man, woman, boy, and girl has been made in the image of God, made for intimacy within God's community and for impact on his mission. We also learned that our rebellion has ruined and misdirected our innate desire to be someone special and do something special (Deuteronomy 32:4-6). What the people at our "tables" need most is a reconciliation to God that will restore in them the image of God (2 Corinthians 5:17-20). They, like us, need adoption through Jesus into God's community-on-mission. By embracing the message of the cross they too can become forgiven sons of the Father, Jesus' family and friends, a people formed by the Holy Spirit into suffering servants. We know that we have been called to sow the seeds of that message, but like the disciples before Pentecost we must also be seekers, waiting in prayer on the Spirit to empower our service (Acts 1:4-2:41).

Our friends Ned and Anna are both people of prayer, and passionate for those in their section of tables. When a Chinese couple moved in a few houses down, Ned and Anna, who have a deep love for internationals, introduced themselves. They also began to seek God and sow good works. It wasn't long before this couple showed up at our church-plant meetings and we began to pray publicly about their desire to stay in the States and become citizens. After months of seeking God in prayer in our gatherings, they announced one Sunday that they had received permission to stay in the US. They thanked us for praying and specifically attributed the good news to our prayers. These folks still don't profess Christ as far as I know, but they had a table for two with a glorious view of the God who answers prayer.

Willing. It has been said that we love to consider ourselves servants until we are treated like such. Serving the needs of others is tedious, tiring, and often thankless work. (Have I mentioned that I don't like serving?) Watching and waiting on the people in our assigned area of influence will require a willingness to sacrifice. Jesus never said this would be easy. In fact he said that serving others "just as I have done to you" (John 13:15) would mean to "deny [your]self and take up [your] cross and follow me" (Matthew 16:24, Mark 8:34, Luke 9:23).

If I have a me-first heart, all I want is to use God, people, and creation to save and serve myself. This makes it impossible for me to bend my heart to the cruciform life, which requires losing my life by using my life to serve God, people, and creation. Serving is sacrifice. To serve is to suffer. I have a friend who serves as the lead discipler of middle-school girls at a large suburban church. Once, while interviewing girls for church membership, it became clear to her that one young lady had no desire to pursue Jesus and was there only to appease her parents. My friend was deeply burdened by this and struggled with how to be a good steward of her relationship with the young lady and her responsibility as a leader. After much prayer and conversation with church leadership, my friend suggested to the girl and her parents that the girl was not yet ready to take membership vows. My friend offered to meet with the young lady for discipleship and conversation, hopeful that the Lord would eventually grab her heart. The parents were outraged, and my faithful friend endured a profanity-laced tongue-lashing over the phone. The family soon left the church, never to be heard from again. A wise woman's loving efforts to protect this young lady from taking vows in vain were met with a verbal assault. I don't know what's become of the girl, by now a young adult, but I do know that through my friend she caught a glimpse of cross-shaped love willing to endure pain in pursuit of a soul that needs Christ.

Welcome. The three activities we've explored — watching, waiting, and being willing — must be supported and surrounded by an attitude and atmosphere of hospitality. Hospitality opens its head, heart, and hands to others, offering help, healing, and hope. Hospitality says, "Welcome." We have been served by One who opened his head, heart, hands, and even his heavenly home not to friends but to foes, not to entertain guests, but in order to give his enemies life by giving up his own. Hospitality is grace, and:

> [G]race is nothing more or less than the face that love wears when it meets imperfection, weakness, failure, sin. Grace is what love is and does when it meets the sinful and undeserving . . . It's what God does when he reaches out in love — sinful as we are — and *welcomes* us into a relationship with himself. [18]

Perhaps you think that serving others is inherently hospitable? But if we serve begrudgingly without the right heart attitude, our service is in vain. A restaurateur observed: "Service you can teach. Hospitality is in you, and it's a born, bred thing more than it's a situation where you can actually train someone to do it."[19] Therein lies our problem. The hospitable, welcoming grace of God is not in us until we are "justified by his grace" and have been adopted as "heirs according to the hope of eternal life." Only then can we and must we "be careful to devote [our]selves to good works" because we have tasted, seen, and are being trained by the grace, the goodness, and loving kindness of God our Savior (Titus 2:11-14, 3:1-10). This attitude of gracious service is only active in the sons of God. I cannot serve unless and until I am a son.

Six

SONS OF GOD

Shaped by the Cross

I knew something was a little off, but until a tour guide pointed to the proof I couldn't quite tell that the Metropolitan Cathedral of Mexico was sinking. A giant plumb-bob had been suspended from the majestic ceiling, its tip hovering centimeters above a square on the floor, allowing engineers to mark the tilting and shifting of the structure over the decades. In fact, the massive cathedral has been gradually slipping into the earth since its construction began more than 400 years ago.

The Mexican government is doing all it can to slow the submersion of Latin America's largest and oldest cathedral, employing every means possible to level out the lopsided landmark. Some small improvements have been made using soil excavation and sunken concrete supports, but even with these successes, the building slowly sinks.

None of the efforts to fix the structure can change the fact that Mexico City was built on a sandy lake bed, leaving nothing solid to support the cathedral. One tourist noted that the plumb-bob markings indicated that the building sinks first on one side and then the other. Decade after decade the plumb-bob has slowly swung back and forth, back and forth, as somewhere deep beneath the surface, individual grains of sand crumble and shift under the structure's immense weight.

That sinking cathedral graphically depicts the condition of many years of my Christian life. Everything looked more or less okay on the surface. The cathedral of my life was full of religious activity, and though I tried everything I could to "be a better Christian," I was sinking. Like that pendulum plumb line I would swing back and forth between religious activity and rebellious apathy. I can't count the number of times that a season of "being good" would be followed by a secret indulgence in "being bad" only to move me into a period of "beating myself up" followed by "trying harder" to make up for "messing up" until I got tired of trying again and turned back to the same old pain relievers. And every time I turned back to sin, the ground underneath me shifted a little.

Three years into marriage and two years into seminary, my self-dependent pursuit of "holiness" and "happiness" came crashing down when a losing battle to secret addictions drove me to the counselor's office. There I found a Christian counselor who knew that the pendulum action of my soul was merely a symptom of the real problem: trying to build my Christian life on the sand of self-dependence instead of Christ the solid rock. I had fallen for the lie that you must trust in Jesus to be saved and then trust yourself to be sanctified (Galatians 3:1-5). So my counselor worked on strengthening the foundation by helping me learn how to live in and by the gospel, not apart from it.

This wise counselor did not ignore my sinful behavior or try to excuse it. Like Jesus, he actually raised the standards of holiness and happiness, helping me see that my violation of the law of love was worse than I thought (Matthew 5:17-30, Romans 13:8-10). He began to open my eyes to my section of tables—specific people in the specific places God had put me to serve: my wife, my fellow seminary students, people at work, and my friends. I wasn't using myself to love and serve the people in my world. I was using the people in my world to love and serve myself.

God began gently to expose the depths of my sin and teach me how to apply the cross to it. He helped me see that my worst sin was the self-dependence of self-righteousness. First, I was depending on myself to love God and others. Then, when I inevitably failed to love, I was depending on my own pursuit of either more performance or more pleasure to alleviate the pain of failure. I learned that the me-first heart, so easy to spot in rebellious perversion, also loves to hide behind religious performance. My counselor encouraged me to take my sinful self-effort to the cross. He encouraged me to embrace the good news that Jesus loved God and others perfectly in my place, that he died to appease God's wrath for my refusal to live for God and others, and that he lives to empower me by his Spirit to live a cross-shaped life.

Two Sons, One Sin

Since then I've found a familiar story told by Jesus to be a powerful metaphor for how living as a son frees me to love as a servant. If you're not acquainted with the parable of the two lost sons, stop for a moment and read Luke 15:11-32. The story opens with the younger brother who demanded his inheritance and his own life, left his father's house, and wasted his stuff and himself in the pursuit of *depraved pleasure*. But the story is really about *two* lost sons. The older brother was lost, too. Like his brother, he proved he wanted nothing more from his father than his inheritance, but he sought to earn it through *dutiful performance* by staying home and working hard.[20] The two sons shared the same sin: *they forsook feasting on the Father's love to feed their souls on something that could never satisfy their God-given craving to be someone special and do something special.* Though their rejection of the father's love took different forms, at the core both of them rejected the father to pursue a false community and a fabricated mission.

Where have we heard this story before? God's son Adam committed this sin in the garden (Genesis 3:6). This was the sin of God's son Israel in the wilderness after the Exodus (Nehemiah 9:9-17, Psalm 78:21-31). Even as the kingdom was in decline, the children of God continued to refuse their Father's invitation to his feast and chose to "spend [their] money for that which is not bread and [their] labor for that which does not satisfy" (Isaiah 55:1-3). Then, through the prophet Jeremiah, God illustrated the core sin that both younger brothers and older brothers commit: "my people have committed two evils: they have forsaken me, the fountain of living waters, and have hewn out cisterns for themselves, broken cisterns that can hold no water" (Jeremiah 2:13).

The self-indulgent and self-righteous both sate their souls with something less satisfying than the Father's love. One will leave the Father's fountain of love to dig a broken cistern of reckless living, while the other will stay "close by" and dig a broken cistern of "righteous" living. This is my story, too. Neither "being good" nor "being bad" satisfies my soul. I end up empty, until I turn from these broken cisterns and rediscover the fountain of the Father's love in Jesus (John 6:32-35, 7:37-39).[21]

Acceptance and Approval

My hunger and thirst for acceptance and approval is what drove me to seek my Elvis kingdom and what made me scared to death to wait tables at Windy Gap. And it's still a battle. Whenever I tell people that I'm a people-pleaser I make sure to add, "And if that bothers you, I'll try to quit." That's why the Father's words to

Jesus capture my heart: "You are my beloved Son; with you I am well pleased" (Mark 1:11). In sharp contrast to me, Jesus has always lived in the embrace and served from the enjoyment of his Father's acceptance and approval (John 3:35, 5:20, 10:17, 15:9-11, 17:24; Hebrews 12:2).

This is acceptance in its purest form: *You are my beloved son. You belong to me. You are loved. You will always be someone special to me and my family. I'm so glad you are with me in my community.*

This is unadulterated approval: *I am well pleased with you. You bring me joy. I count you good, as my Son is good. I pronounce you holy, as my Son is holy. Empowered by my Spirit, you will always do something special with me and my family. I'm so pleased that you are with me on my mission.*

This is what I long for, and this is what I have in the gospel. As Tullian Tchividjian says, "The gospel tells me my identity and security is [sic] in Christ—this frees me to give everything I have because in Christ I have everything I need." [22] In the life, death, and resurrected life of Jesus Christ, the Father has spread a banquet of grace that strengthens my soul with his acceptance and approval so that I can offer them to the hungry souls in my section of tables.

The Father's Feast

What exactly does the Father serve his sons and daughters at his banqueting table? When Jesus lifted the cup of wine at the first Lord's Supper, he said "this cup is the new covenant in my blood. Do this, as often as you drink it, in remembrance of me" (1 Corinthians 11:25). When we feed on and drink of Jesus by faith in his gospel as it is proclaimed at the communion table, he wants us to remember that through his sacrifice we have inherited the new purity, new passion, new power, and new partnership that his Father promised in the New Covenant (Ezekiel 36:25-28).

A 17th-century pastor, Walter Marshall, wrestled with his inability to live a holy life of loving God and loving others, so he searched the scriptures and sought the counsel of godly men until he learned "four things God must give you if you are going to live a holy life."[23] These four happen to correspond with the four promises of the New Covenant (aka the gospel) which are ours as we embrace the cross of Christ as ours. [24] Let's revisit these four ideas from Chapter Two, this time at perhaps a different level of understanding.

Four Needs, Four Gifts

<u>A New Purity.</u> The first thing God must give us if we are going to live a holy life is purity. Walter Marshall put it this way: "You have to be totally assured that you are reconciled to God and accepted by him. You have to be absolutely sure that the chasm sin has caused between you and God has been completely filled, and that you are now totally under his love and favor."[25] This purity that we need to be assured of was accomplished when the promise of Ezekiel 36:25 came true

in Christ, "I will sprinkle clean water on you, and you shall be clean from all your uncleannesses, and from all your idols I will cleanse you."

> *When I first feasted by faith on Jesus' sacrifice, I received the Father's **acceptance** because my disobedience was paid for, and I received his **approval** because the perfect obedience (righteousness) he requires of me was provided for me by Jesus. This occurs because of what the Bible calls **justification**: my sins are pardoned, so I'm accepted; I have the Son's perfect record, so I'm approved. I am pure: a gift from God.*

A New Passion. The second thing God must give us is passion, or what Marshall calls willingness and ability to obey God: "Your heart has to be freely motivated to obey God's Law. . . . You must have a total inward inclination to want to obey God and to avoid sin."[26] This is not something we could ever produce by ourselves, so God made it possible by fulfilling in Christ the promise of Ezekiel 36:26, "And I will give you a new heart, and a new spirit I will put within you. And I will remove the heart of stone from your flesh and give you a heart of flesh."

When by grace our faith is awakened and we are empowered to grab hold of the message of the cross, God gives us the Spirit of his Son through **adoption**. Through the Spirit we, like Jesus, can cry out "Abba, Father!" (Galatians 4:6, Romans 8:14-16)

Think about that. We who once were children of

wrath with hearts enslaved and inclined to sin, now
have the same desire to obey our Father that Jesus has
(Galatians 4:7-9, 5:13-15). This is not to say that obedience
is our only desire, for in this life we are frail and fallen
creatures subject to temptation. But every true child of
God can sense that desire to obey the Father, a desire
that cannot be present apart from salvation. Through
the gospel we get a heart transplant. God replaces the
me-first hearts of his adopted sons with the you-first
heart of his only-begotten Son (2 Corinthians 5:21).

> *When I continue to feed by faith on Jesus' sacrifice,
> I live sensing the Father's* **acceptance** *because the
> Holy Spirit pours the Father's love into me, con-
> vincing me that I am free from sin by the grace of
> God—no longer ashamed, but hopeful* (Romans 5:5),
> *no longer dead, but alive* (Romans 6:11), *no longer a
> slave, but a son* (Romans 8:15-16). *This gives me a new
> Godward passion.*

A New Power. The third gift God must give us is
the power to continue obeying God. Walter Marshall
writes, "You have to be totally assured that you have
sufficient strength both to *will* and to *do* what God
calls you to do.... God wants you to know that you
have the power from him to live a holy life."[27] God did
this for us by fulfilling Ezekiel 36:27: "I will put my
Spirit in you and will *cause you* to walk in my statutes
and be careful to obey my rules."

> *As I feast by faith on Jesus' sacrifice in an ongoing
> way, I continue to receive the Father's* **approval**

> *because the Holy Spirit puts the life of Jesus in me
> and gradually conforms me to the image of Jesus the
> Servant, so that I might live and love like him by the
> power of the Spirit* (Galatians 2:20; Ephesians 1:19-20, 3:16,
> 20; 2 Corinthians 3:18). *This is what the Bible calls **sanc-
> tification**: "Sanctification is the work of God's free
> grace by which our whole person is made new in the
> image of God, and we are made more and more able
> to become dead to sin and alive to righteousness."[28]*

A New Partnership. The fourth and final gift God
must give us in order for us to be able to live a holy life
is partnership with God for the future. Again, we read
from Walter Marshall:

> You have to be absolutely assured that you are
> going to have a happy, eternal future with the
> Lord in the new heaven and earth.... If there is no
> eternal future with the Lord, why would anyone
> choose suffering for Christ rather than sin?...
> God uses the sure hope of the glory of heaven
> to encourage his people to obey him (Hebrews
> 6:11-12, 12:2; 1 John 3:1-3).

This gift from God is promised to us throughout
Scripture, but especially fittingly as part of the New
Covenant: "You shall dwell in the land that I gave to
your fathers, and you shall be my people, and I will
be your God" (Ezekiel 36:28). Through the gospel we are
restored to a new partnership with the Father and the

Son, by the Spirit, in the family business of reconciliation, living and serving with him forever, and "making all things new" (2 Corinthians 5:17-21, Revelation 21:1-5, Ephesians 1:22-23, Colossians 1:19-20).

> *The ultimate fulfillment of this promised new partnership is reserved for the new heaven and earth in that "happily ever after" part of our story that the Bible calls **glorification** (Romans 8:29-30).[29] But as I continue to feast on the gifts of the Father in this life, through the process of sanctification the Spirit progressively transforms me by the gospel. This enables me increasingly to live out here and now the glorious partnership that will be perfectly and permanently ours then and there* (2 Corinthians 3:17-18, Philippians 3:20).[30]

Table Talk

There I sat in the pew one particular Sunday, holding the communion wafer and the tiny plastic cup of juice. That's when the beatings began. As the organist played a familiar hymn softly and others received their own wafers and juice, I launched into my ritual of self-condemnation, beating myself up for this or that sin while a vision of the Father's frowning face danced mockingly in my head. Suddenly a memory of something that happened the night before burst through the dark clouds in my heart. I remembered quietly opening the door to my two-year-old twins' bedroom. I stood there for a moment watching them sleep sweetly, a thumb in the mouth of one and two fingers in the mouth of the other. A tidal wave of love and joy flooded my soul as I watched them. *These are my beloved twins, in whom I delight.* Back in the pew now, I was overwhelmed with the Father's desire for and delight in me.

This is how I look at you and feel about you, Jimmy! You are my beloved son in whom I am well pleased because of Jesus. That's what this table, this feast, is about. Yes, you should recognize that your sin is what made the sacrifice of Jesus necessary, but remember: "For every one look at your sin, take ten looks at Jesus," and "there is more mercy in Christ than there is sin in you."[31] *Fellowship with me at this feast, my son. There is no condemnation for those who are in Christ Jesus. You have my acceptance and my approval. Live in them.*

Seven
EMBRACING THE GOSPEL

Taking In the Cross

I was once asked in a youth-ministry job interview about the current state of my spiritual disciplines. I admitted sheepishly that I was inconsistent in my daily devotions. I said that I was "taking a break" from spiritual disciplines because my "personal time with God" had slipped across that fuzzy line between loving devotion and legalistic duty. Not my best foot forward, but at least I was being honest.

The truth is, after more than thirty years of walking with Jesus, my pattern in regard to devotions has been a predictable one:

1) Pursue prayer and Bible study with Spirit-driven get-to-meet-with-God energy.

2) Watch that energy slowly dissolve into self-dependent ought-to-have-my-quiet-time effort.

3) Eventually give in to what's-the-use apathy.

4) Regroup and pick it up again at step one.

In other words, I swing back and forth in the discipline of daily devotions between self-righteous effort and self-indulgent laziness. Both extremes are pure legalism. I've thought about visiting a Legalists Anonymous meeting, but I'm afraid they'd expect me to attend religiously.

Spiritual Formation Happens

God never changes, but we change all the time. We are not only *capable* of being molded, we are *given* to being molded. For better or worse, we're all being shaped *by* something into the shape *of* something all the time. C. S. Lewis said it best in *Mere Christianity*:

> And taking your life as a whole, with all your innumerable choices, all your life long you are slowly turning this central [part of you] either into a heavenly creature or into a hellish creature: either into a creature that is in harmony with God, and with other creatures, and with itself, or else into one that is in a state of war and hatred with God, and with its fellow-creatures, and with itself. . . . Each of us at each moment is progressing to the one state or the other. [32]

So we need discipline to pursue the heavenly formation. "Discipline," according to Jerry Bridges, "refers to certain activities designed to train a person in a particular skill." [33] Psychologists will tell you that everything we do is a kind of training, and in a sense that's true. Everything that you and I desire, think, say, listen to, watch, read, or choose comes together to form a pattern of activities training us to live either a hellish me-first or a heavenly you-first life. This pattern is largely made up of a set of "disciplines" that you and I practice over and over again, consciously or not. They may not feel like spiritual disciplines, but they are forming our souls. The decision is not whether you will or won't practice spiritual disciplines, but rather what sort of disciplines you will *prefer* to practice. "Holiness is not a condition into which we drift," [34] so we have to choose the pattern of disciplines that will train us in the skill of holy living and wholly loving.

One simple statement made by a retreat leader several years ago gave me hope that I could pursue Christian spiritual disciplines from a heart of desire, not duty. Our church's youth ministry staff was taking a weekend away to learn more about the validity and variety of spiritual disciplines practiced throughout the history of the church. Anxiety welled up in me as the retreat leader told us we would spend two days practicing journaling, solitude and silence, and all sorts of prayer and Bible reading. Fear of falling back into legalism gripped me, until he explained, "I don't practice these disciplines to *get* God to love me, but to hear him say it." That one little side comment completely changed my understanding of the purpose of the spiritual disciplines.

The Purpose of Cross-Shaped Disciplines

At one particular point in my life I realized I had been practicing "cross-less devotions." I was working hard at spending time with God while forgetting the very gospel that permits and prompts me to do so. We are not to practice Bible reading, fasting, solitude, prayer, and other disciplines to *make* God happy with us but to *make space* to *hear* how happy God is with us because of Jesus. When I have a quiet time in order to get God to love me, I am a legalist who "slaves away" to earn the favor of God, not a loved son who enjoys fellowship with his Father.

The purpose of spiritual disciplines is to make room in my life to "repent and believe in the gospel" (Mark 1:15), to forsake my broken cisterns and drink again from "the fountain of living waters" (Jeremiah 2:13). Cross-shaped spiritual disciplines enable me to hear God the Father say that I already have his acceptance and approval through God the Son, so that I can now work with him in the resurrection power that God the Spirit supplies. I cannot *earn* the presence and power of God in my life by saying and doing the right things. Practicing the spiritual disciplines enables me to *enter* God's presence and *engage* his power by *embracing* the good news that Jesus has already said and done the right things for me. When my spiritual disciplines are shaped by the cross, then whatever spiritual discipline I practice, my aim is the same: to feed by faith on Jesus Christ as he is offered in the gospel. Rephrase my retreat leader to think about your own spiritual practices: "I don't _____ (pray, read my Bible, fast, etc.) to *get* the Father to love me. I _____ to hear him say he loves me in the gospel of his Son, Jesus Christ."

The Power of Cross-Shaped Disciplines

Paul understood that the power to live like Christ comes from believing the promise that we are loved by Christ. That's why he said, "I live *by faith* in the Son of God, who *loved me* and *gave himself for me*" (Galatians 2:20). Living by faith in the gospel, Paul drew upon the love of Christ to gain strength to live like Christ.

Right after he wrote these words, Paul addressed the issue that made him so angry with the Galatians. They had begun their Christian lives by embracing the gospel. Then they experienced the power of the Holy Spirit to obey. But now they were pursuing cross-less obedience in their own strength. Paul's remedy? Look to the cross and you'll live by the Spirit.

> O foolish Galatians! Who has bewitched you? It was before your eyes that Jesus Chris was publicly portrayed as crucified. Let me ask you only this: Did you receive the Spirit by works of the law or by hearing with faith? Are you so foolish?

Having begun by the Spirit, are you now being perfected by the flesh? Did you suffer so many things in vain—if indeed it was in vain? Does he who supplies the Spirit to you and works miracles among you do so by works of the law, or by hearing with faith (Galatians 3:1-5).

The power to serve God and others in my section of tables flows from the Holy Spirit when I grip the gospel by faith. Here's the process I see in Galatians 3:1-5:

The gospel proclaimed (v 1)

+

The gospel heard and embraced by faith (v 2, 5)

=

Obedience (thus gradually "being perfected") by the power of the Spirit (v 3-5)

"*By hearing with faith* is not only the way to start the Christian life but is also the way to continue it day by day."[35] The spiritual disciplines are the means by which I am reminded that the New Covenant promises of a new purity, passion, power, and partnership have been bought for me by the love of Jesus poured out on the cross. Pastor Marshall explains how:

The blessings of your holy nature will empower you to love and obey God. You can only live out of your new nature when you live by faith. Particularly, you must believe that all your sins are blotted out, that you are reconciled to God, that you have access into his favor by the blood of Christ, that God is your Father, that he loves you, and that you have all you need for your eternal happiness in Christ.

If you meditate on these wonderful truths of the gospel, God will be very lovely to your heart. These precious truths will sweetly draw you and win you over. You will not be forced to "love God" by commands or threats. You will love God because these precious realities of the gospel will draw you to love God. If you truly want to love God, you cannot harbor the secret suspicion that he is really your everlasting enemy. [36]

If the love of Christ is what compels us to "no longer live for [ourselves] but for him who for [our] sake died and was raised" (2 Corinthians 5:14-15), then we must continually abide in his love to bear the fruit of love (John 15:1-11).

The Practice of Cross-Shaped Disciplines

The gospel has begun to transform the way I practice the spiritual disciplines.

<u>Bible.</u> Now I read, study, memorize, and meditate on the Bible because I want to *love*, *learn*, and *live in* the story of Jesus.

- I use Bible-reading plans to get a continual overview of the *drama* unfolded in the Old and New Testaments so that I will *love* the story of Jesus.
- I study *doctrine* (or theology) because it helps answer big questions about God, people, and the world that enable me to better *learn* the story of Jesus.
- I look for all the ways I'm commanded to repent of sin, believe the gospel, and love God and people because these *directions* tell me how to *live in* the story of Jesus as part of his community on his mission.

Prayer. Prayer, whether scheduled or spontaneous, declares my dependence on God. Prayerlessness, on the other hand, declares the felt independence of a me-first heart. Jerry Bridges explains,

> We may assent to the fact that we depend on Christ, but if our prayer life is meager or perfunctory, we thereby deny it. We are in effect saying that we can handle most of our spiritual life with our own self-discipline and our perceived innate goodness. Or perhaps we are saying we are not even committed to the pursuit of holiness. [37]

When I refuse to pray, I refuse to believe the gospel. I once heard Larry Crabb say, "If I'm going to live like a man, I'm going to have to pray like a little boy."[38]

When I pray, I join my Father at the family table. Like a little boy, I get to talk to my Father about the highs and lows of my day, my heart's joys and sorrows. I can ask him for what I think I need while recognizing that as a wise Father he will "only give me what I would have asked for if I knew all that he knows."[39] This kind of "relational prayer," as Crabb calls it, is cross-shaped because it "provides the Spirit with a wide open opportunity to do what he loves most to do, to draw me into the heart and life of the Father and to make me more like the Son."[40] If I'm going to live like a servant, I'm going to have to pray like a son. Perhaps that's why the original Son-Servant taught us to pray as he prays, "Our Father . . ." (Matthew 6:9-13).

Fasting, Solitude, Silence. Sometimes I need to practice disciplines that will expose the broken cisterns I tend to drink from, when I ought to be drinking from the fountain of my Father's love (Jeremiah 2:13).

- *Fasting* from food or caffeine, from books or music, from talk radio, from Facebook or Twitter, or from any number of other comforts helps me see whether I've been depending on the *stuff* God has given me more than I have been depending on his Spirit.
- *Solitude* is a temporary fast from people I may depend on more than Jesus.
- *Silence* is a fast from my own words and the messages of the world in order to retrain my heart to hear by faith the message of the cross.

Most of these things are good gifts from my Father, but these forms of fasting help me discern whether I trust the gifts more than the Giver. When I practice these disciplines, both the pervasive nature of my sin and my profound need for my Savior are more clearly revealed, affording me the opportunity to feed more fully on Jesus as he offers himself in the gospel.

Public Worship. We don't often think of public worship as a spiritual discipline, but it too makes space for us to practice the disciplines of grace in a cross-shaped community for the sake of cross-shaped mission. In public worship we hear the gospel *together* through the preaching of God's Word; we depend on God's grace *together* by praying corporately; and we let go of our time, treasure, and talents *together* by sacrificially sharing our gifts.

In corporate worship we can partake of two of God's most powerful means of grace: baptism and the Lord's Supper. As for *baptism*, Pastor Marshall's instruction is helpful, even to those baptized long ago: "Stir yourself up and strengthen yourself by your baptism. Lay hold of the grace that it seals to you, and fulfill what it calls you to be and do before God – to live as one who has died and risen with Christ. . . . Baptism points you to the central truths of the gospel."[41]

Marshall is equally helpful here:

The sacrament of the Lord's Supper is a spiritual feast to nourish your faith . . . a wonderful, symbolic picture of the fact that you must constantly live upon a crucified Savior . . . also a precious means by which Christ, the bread and drink of life, is really given to you. . . . Christ is spiritually [not physically] present in the Lord's Supper. You receive him, through faith, when you partake of it! [42]

The Problem with Cross-less Disciplines

Spiritual disciplines have long been called a "means of grace," a means to a particular end. By means of the spiritual disciplines we live by faith in the Son of God. The end we pursue is that we might love God and others in the power of his Spirit (2 Corinthians 13:14, Titus 3:4-8). The problem is that spiritual disciplines can easily become the end and not the means. This happens when the disciplines become cross-less rituals and routines rather than cross-centered resources for renewal.[43] Too often I settle for going through the motions of Bible reading or prayer, making them merely empty activities on my daily agenda. Or I turn the disciplines into idols, functional "saviors" that I depend on more than Jesus, somehow believing they will sanctify me apart from the gospel. As we practice these disciplines we must keep in mind that "In themselves they do not make you holy; they draw you into fellowship with Christ, the True Vine, who makes you holy as you abide in him."[44]

Let's zoom in on the Celtic cross diagram and

focus on the cross in the middle that represents our dependence on the gospel.

The spiritual disciplines (partially represented here by the words "Bible," "Prayer," "Worship," and "Fasting") are the means by which we feast on our Father's love as we repent and believe the good news of his Son's sacrifice. As a result, we are strengthened for service in his Kingdom.

Helping Myself . . . To the Father's Feast

I'm beginning to learn to use the Bible, prayer, fasting, and public worship to repent of my self-righteousness and to believe ever more deeply the good news that Jesus is righteous for me and that he will express his righteousness through me by the power of his Spirit. I am finding these words from John Piper to be true: "Hearing the word of the cross, and preaching it to ourselves, is the central strategy for sinners in the fight for joy. Nothing works without this. Here is where we start. And here is where we stay. We never outgrow the gospel."[45]

Rather than use self-dependent discipline to help myself obey, I'm learning to use Spirit-dependent disciplines to help myself to the gospel. Our Father invites us to a feast!

Eight
EXPRESSING THE GOSPEL

Taking Up Your Cross

Thursday, June 19, 1997 threw everything I knew about being God's beloved son and blessed servant into question. My wife, Christine, and I were 10 months into my first full-time youth-ministry position. The week before I had led our students on a missions trip, and had just wrapped up day four of a frantic week of Vacation Bible School. We had decided to relax with dinner and a movie at home that evening, and I had gone to the store to buy a few things we needed for the meal. Twenty minutes later, when I pulled into our driveway, a blast of flame filled the sun porch, off the kitchen. I leaped from the car and bolted toward the house as the sound of Christine's screams filled my ears.

When I ripped open the door to the sun porch, everything seemed to shift into slow motion. Maneuvering past furniture wrapped in tight coats of flame, I slipped and fell. It took a long time to get to the floor.

I was lying in a warm, wet slime. Then I remembered. Christine was trying a new recipe and had put a pot of grease on the stove just before I left. I noticed a low, blue flame all around me, covering the porch and the kitchen floor. I picked up a burning throw rug and began to beat at the flames.

After a few moments I abandoned the task, drawn by Christine's screams of agony and alarm. Mostly agony. It seemed she was outside now. As I ran back out the door to find her, a neighbor asked how he could help. I told him to use my garden hose to put out the porch fire.

As I rounded the front of the house, Christine was pacing frantically on the front walk, screaming and crying as the skin fell off her arms and legs in sheets. Her beautiful blond hair was singed and her face bright red with first degree burns. I wanted desperately to act but stood frozen in place, paralyzed by shock and an overwhelming helplessness.

The neighbor who had offered to help was a doctor. He sat my stunned wife on the front porch and carefully ran cool water from the hose over her blistered arms and legs. He gently removed the watch and rings from her scorched left hand and slipped off the socks that held scalding grease against her feet and toes.

Within minutes emergency personnel arrived to care for Christine and extinguish the small fire. My wife was rushed to Baptist Hospital and, after a quick assessment, taken by helicopter to the USA Medical Center in nearby Mobile, Alabama. She would remain there for 31 days, having suffered burns over 38 percent of her body.

Alone in my car, following the ambulance to Baptist Hospital, I pounded my fist on the dashboard, shouting, "God, I don't like this! I don't like this at all!" The past six years of marriage flashed across my mind. Christine already suffered much from chronic migraines, fibromyalgia, and the soul-ache of postponing her dreams of motherhood while working full-time to put me through seminary.

In the face of these challenges we had weathered several years of intense counseling. Now, finally, seminary was over, I was in ministry, and we were growing as husband and wife. Although ready to begin a family, we were now seeking medical help to resolve infertility problems, and Christine was facing the pain and fear of possibly never being a mom. Only days before she had wondered out loud if all of this hurt and struggle might mean God had abandoned her. Now this?

"How could you do this to her?" I growled at God through clenched teeth. "She has been faithful to you! Is this how you show your daughter your love? Is this how you show *me* your love?" After my sobs subsided I remembered Jesus' question to his remaining followers after "many of his disciples turned back and no longer walked with him . . . *'Do you want to go away as well?'"* (John 6:66-67). "Where else can I go?" I cried, "Only you have the life I need" (John 6:68-69). "And I need you right now."

Schooled by Suffering

Soon after Christine's accident, someone commented cheerfully, "I can't wait to hear what God teaches you through all of this." While she might have carried out her good intentions with a little more sensitivity, she spoke truth. God was teaching us. He is always teaching all his children. I don't want to oversimplify, or suggest we can always know the precise purpose behind every challenge and trial, but I do think we can make some informed, helpful, biblical generalizations.

God's lessons are not a me-first self-improvement program challenging me to buckle down and try harder to be a better Christian. No, in the Father's School of Suffering every lesson has one basic aim: that we might repent and believe the gospel (Mark 1:14-15, John 6:28-29, 1 John 3:23). First comes our one-time, definitive repentance and believing unto a salvation that can never and will never be taken from us. But then comes our continual repentance and believing unto sanctification, a transformation that will not end until we leave these bodies. God, our all-wise instructor, knows that only the foundation of the gospel, of turning from sin and trusting Jesus, will support the cruciform cathedral of loving God and others that we are to build (Matthew 7:24; 1 Corinthians 3:11-17; Hebrews 6:1-2, 9-12; Titus 2:11-14).

That summer night in 1997, the Father was intensifying his gracious training of our hearts in two ways. He was calling us to a deeper dependence on his love by embracing the gospel as his *beloved son and daughter*. And he was preparing us to live as his *blessed servants*, equipped and empowered to offer his love in our section of tables as Seekers, Shepherds, Sowers, and Stewards.

Beloved Son and Daughter

"As I fought for my life and struggled with faith," Christine would later write about her time in the Burn Unit, "God whispered his promises to me, 'Do not fear, for I have redeemed you. I have called you by name; you are mine! For I am the Lord your God – the Holy One of Israel, your Savior!' But along with the comfort of these verses came confusion. How could God say, 'When you walk through the fire you shall not be burned; the flames will not consume you'?

"As God gradually healed my wounds, he also continued to speak to my heart. I saw with fresh eyes that God knows his people by name and has made a special covenant with us. This covenant does not promise a life free of floodwaters and fire, but it does promise that nothing will *overcome* us—and I was not overcome. God doesn't promise protection from physical pain, but he does promise that he will be with us (Isaiah 43:2, 5)—and he was with me. God will love us because we are precious to him (Isaiah 43:4), and he will always bring us back to himself (Isaiah 43:4-7). I have walked through the fire and have smelled the stench of charred skin, but I have also tasted the goodness of God's love."[46]

As for me, my first reaction to Christine's accident—*Is this how you show your love to those who dedicate their lives to serve you?*—recalls an observation Jerry Bridges has made:

> [We Christians] tend to base our relationship with God on our performance instead of on his grace. If we've performed well—whatever "well" is in our opinion—then we expect God to bless us. If we haven't done so well, our expectations are reduced accordingly. In this sense, we live by works, rather than by grace. [47]

For both Christine and me, the trial that at first seemed to disprove our sonship and make a mockery of the Father's love for us eventually became a fresh affirmation of both sonship and love.

> For the Lord disciplines the one he loves, and chastises every son whom he receives ... God is treating you as sons. For what son is there whom his father does not discipline? If you are left without discipline, in which all have participated, then you are illegitimate children and not sons"
> (Hebrews 12:6-8, see also Proverbs 3:11-12, Psalm 94:12, Revelation 3:19).

Such painful training is loving because God's ultimate goal is to make his adopted sons like his Son Jesus. "He disciplines us for our good, that we may share his *holiness*. For the moment all discipline seems painful rather than pleasant, but later it yields the peaceful fruit of *righteousness* to those who have been trained by it" (Hebrews 12:10b-11).

Suffering for the Christian is neither the result of God's punishment nor a sign of his rejection. The word *discipline* is used to indicate training, growth, improvement, advancement. It is for our *good*, an essential part of the continual redirection of our hearts away from our own me-first path and back onto God's you-first path. Those who have been born anew into Christ's kingdom must take up their crosses and die daily to their me-first hearts, following the one who took up his cross and "learned obedience through what he suffered" (Hebrews 5:8, see also Luke 9:23-25, Hebrew 2:10, Philippians 2:8).

We must endure—and by grace we can and will endure—whatever means God may choose in order to do us good through discipline. Part of the wonder of our salvation is that for each of us there is a unique and fore-ordained plan (the farthest possible thing from a series of random or pointless circumstances) by which God is committed to seeing us live a cross-shaped life (Hebrews 12:3-7a).

So, how does suffering reveal our Father's love? God uses suffering to loosen our grip on the lies we've embraced, and to implant in us his words of truth, revealing to us the depth of that truth at levels we could never glimpse in the absence of suffering.

Our heavenly Father allows suffering to train his children because, though he loves us as we are, he loves us too much to leave us as we are. He wants more for us than "good enough Christianity."[48] He wants us to more fully *embrace* Jesus through the gospel so that we might more fully *express* Jesus by sharing and showing the gospel to a world hungry for truth.

Blessed Servants

God's School of Suffering is a vocational school. Here we are apprenticed to Jesus to learn alongside him how to fulfill our calling to love God, people, and all of creation as Seekers, Shepherds, Stewards, and Sowers.

Seekers

I relocated to Mobile for the duration of Christine's treatment. During our month there she had two major surgeries. One was a skin-graft procedure that involved harvesting healthy skin from her back, thighs, and abdomen and using it to cover the 38 percent of her body that had been burned. The second was a skin graft for her left hand and the amputation of two toes that were beyond repair. Before each surgery and throughout the painful recoveries, Christine and I sought the Lord by singing a praise song based on Isaiah 43 — a song we had learned on our youth missions trip, one week before the fire:

When you walk through the fire, you'll not be
burned
And the flames, they will not consume
Do not fear, for I will be with you
I have called you by name, you are mine
For I am the Lord your God
I am the Lord your God,
the Holy One of Israel, your Savior
I am the Lord, do not fear [49]

We believe God gave us the gift of his Word
wrapped in a song, at just that point in our lives, to
remind us of the promises Jesus bought for us with his
blood, and to help us learn to seek him, his kingdom,
and his righteousness in all circumstances (Matthew 6:33).
Gospel-soaked songs remain vital to our family as we
continue to learn to seek the Lord and his presence
continually (Psalm 105:4).

Shepherds and Sowers

During our hospital stay, I heard Christine share her
story and her Savior's love with the teenage girl in
the Burn Unit bed beside her, as well as with nurses,
doctors, and physical therapists. In the years since then
God has used Christine's story of pain and her gospel-
transformed heart to shepherd suffering Christian
women and to sow the good news about our Savior in
the lives of women who don't yet know him. She and
several of her friends lead retreats for Christian women.

They get to know the unique journeys and wounds of these women, helping them to hear the voice of the Shepherd and follow him more closely. Christine and her friends help these women discover the green pastures of God's Word and cool waters of prayer. They have taken this same ministry to Africa, sowing works of service and words of witness to broken women who need to know there is a Good Shepherd who is also the Lamb of God who takes away the sin of the world.

Stewards

This traumatic event was a wake-up call for Christine and I to be stewards for the sake of God's kingdom. We were reminded to hold loosely and lovingly the people and things we had once hugged with an idolatrous embrace. Christine would tell you that her body, her appearance, was an idol to her, a functional savior on which she relied for acceptance and approval. Today there is almost no place on her that has not been scarred either by the burns or the skin grafts, a fitting reminder that her body is not her own, but has been bought with a price and branded with the glory of a nail-scarred Savior (1 Corinthians 6:19-20).

Christine would also tell you that my ministry was more important to me than our marriage. Working for God had become my counterfeit god. But from the moment Christine was burned, I dropped everything for thirty-one days. Suddenly I was willing to risk losing my job because I had almost lost my wife. In a huge demonstration of grace, our church was more than generous. They gave me the time off, cleaned and repaired the fire damage to our home, took care of our pets, and filled in for me in the youth ministry. That month I began to learn to be a faithful steward of the first ministry God had given me: my marriage. To this day, Christine says that this chapter in our story finally calmed her nagging fear that I might not really love her. Our walk through the fire challenged us both to be stewards, to stop relying on our God-given resources as idols to serve our me-first selves, and to begin to use our resources as tools to serve God and others with you-first hearts.

The Glory of God's Cruciform Community

This season of suffering also gave us a front-row seat to the glory of God on display in his cruciform community, the church. We heard stories about the body of Christ seeking God on our behalf all over the world. We were shepherded by hundreds of letters, cards, calls, and visits. As good stewards of God's grace our congregation prayed fervently for Christine, set up an assistance fund to help with bills, signed up for shifts to drive her to and from physical therapy appointments, and countless other acts of hospitality (see 1 Peter 4:9-11). Christine was cared for by other believers who were fulfilling their calling as sowers by serving in the medical profession. Christine's surgeon was a former missionary. A nurse who knows Jesus well encouraged me with his grace during Christine's twice daily wound-care treatments. The Christian occupational therapist who is responsible for Christine's ability to use her left hand became a dear sister to her during the months of therapy that followed our return home. The care we received from God's people far and near made Paul's words about the body of Christ come alive: "If one member suffers, all suffer together" (1 Corinthians 12:26a).

All of God's people are called to full-time ministry, the ministry of displaying the glory of Christ as cruciform cathedrals in the midst of a world that needs him. John Piper said it well:

> God intends for the afflictions of Christ to be presented to the world through the afflictions of his people. God really means for the body of Christ, the church, to experience some of the suffering he experienced so that when we proclaim the cross as the way to life, people will see the marks of the cross in us and feel the love of the cross from us. Our calling is to make the afflictions of Christ real for people by the afflictions we experience in bringing them the message of salvation. [50]

Sons and Daughters

Until Jesus returns for that great graduation day, class is still in session. We are continuing to learn what it means to truly live as his beloved children and blessed servants. And as good teachers do, he changes up the curriculum now and then, sometimes choosing to train us by joy. Exactly one year to the day of Christine's accident, June 19, 1998, we discovered by ultrasound that she was pregnant with twins. God in his kindness redeemed that day of pain for his son and daughter, transforming it into a day of joy. Eventually we learned the twins were a girl and boy, Abi and Micah. Three and a half years later he would add Anna to our family. Now the Davis family celebrates "Life Day" every year on June 19. Christine gets five roses, one for each life now part of our family. God spared her life that day and gave three new lives to us in the days that followed. Yes, we're still learning what it means to be God's children, but now we have a son and daughters of our own. Enrolled now in the School of Parenting, the lessons are still the same: the Father continues to teach us to embrace his love in Christ through the gospel so that we will express his love through the gospel of Christ to the world. We'll spend the rest of our lives being and making cruciform disciples of our crucified Lord.

Further Reading

Introduction

Unfashionable: Making a Difference in the World by being Different, TullianTchividjian

Restoring Broken Things: What Happens When We Catch a Vision of the New World Jesus is Creating, Steven Curtis Chapman and Scotty Smith

Recovering the Real Lost Gospel: Reclaiming the Gospel as Good News, Darrell Bock

Chapter One—Created to be Cruciform

Heaven Is A Place on Earth: Why Everything You Do Matters to God, Michael Wittmer

Learning God's Story of Grace, Elizabeth Reynolds Turnage

A Quest for More: Living for Something Bigger than You, Paul David Tripp

Chapter Two—Redeemed to be Cruciform

God's Big Picture: Tracing the Storyline of the Bible, Vaughn Roberts

The God Who Is There: Finding Your Place in God's Story, D. A. Carson

66 Love Letters: A Conversation with God That Invites You into His Story, Larry Crabb

I Will Be Your God: How God's Covenant Enriches Our Lives, T. M. Moore

Chapter Three—The Elements of Being Cruciform

The Gospel for Real Life: Turning to the Liberating Power of the Cross Everyday, Jerry Bridges

Renewal as a Way of Life, Richard Lovelace

The Gospel-Driven Life: Being Good News People in a Bad News World, Michael Horton

Chapter Four—The Cruciform Life in Action

Experiencing the Trinity, Darrell W. Johnson

Living the Cross-Centered Life, C. J. Mahaney

The Gospel-Centered Life: A Nine Lesson Study, World Harvest Mission

Gospel Transformation, World Harvest Mission

Chapter Five — Servants of God: In the Shape of the Cross

Servanthood As Worship: The Privilege of Life in a Local Church, Nate Palmer

Generous Justice: How God's Grace Makes Us Just, Tim Keller

The Insider: Bringing the Kingdom of God into Your Everyday World, Jim Petersen and Mike Shamy

The Master Plan of Evangelism, Robert E. Coleman

Chapter Six — Sons of God: Shaped by the Cross

Prodigal God: Recovering the Heart of the Christian Faith, Timothy Keller

Reclaiming Adoption: Missional Living through the Rediscovery of Abba Father, Dan Cruver, John Piper, Scotty Smith, Richard D. Phillips, and Jason Kovacs

Desiring God: Meditations of a Christian Hedonist, John Piper

Inside Out, Larry Crabb

Chapter Seven — Embracing the Gospel: Taking in the Cross

The Discipline of Grace: God's Role and Our Role in the Pursuit of Holiness, Jerry Bridges

When I Don't Desire God: How to Fight for Joy, John Piper

A Hunger for God: Desiring God through Fasting and Prayer, John Piper

The Bookends of the Christian Life, Jerry Bridges and Bob Bevington

The Gospel Mystery of Sanctification, Walter Marshall (A New Version put into Modern English by Bruce McRae)

Spiritual Disciplines for the Christian Life, Donald Whitney

Chapter Eight — Expressing the Gospel: Taking Up Your Cross

When God Weeps: Why Our Sufferings Matter to the Almighty, Joni Eareckson Tada and Steve Estes

A Praying Life: Connecting with God in a Distracting World, Paul Miller

Wrestling with an Angel: A Story of Love, Disability and the Lessons of Grace, Greg Lucas

Finding God and Shattered Dreams, Larry Crabb

Endnotes

1. *Unfashionable* (Multnomah, 2009), 44. Bible teachers differ on the number of "acts" that tell the biblical story. I've seen a range from three to six "acts" proposed, but they all include the three that I have here. The most common version, and the one I usually prefer, is four acts: Creation, Fall, Redemption, and Restoration (or Consummation). For the sake of brevity in this short book, I've collapsed Redemption and Restoration into one act.

2. The *ESV Study Bible* note on Genesis 2:15 explains: "The overall picture of Eden presented in the preceding verses suggests that the park-like garden is part of a divine sanctuary. **The man is put** in the garden **to work it and keep it**}. The term 'work' (Hb. ['abad]; cf. v 5; 3:23; 4:2, 12; Proverbs. 12:11; 28:19) denotes preparing and tending, and 'keep' (Hb. shamar) adds to that idea. . . . Later, the same two verbs are used together of the work undertaken by the priests and Levites in the tabernacle ('minister' or 'serve' [Hb. 'abad] and 'guard' [Hb. [shamar]]; e.g., Numbers 3:7–8, 18:7). The man's role is to be not only a gardener but also a guardian. As a priest, he is to maintain the sanctity of the garden as part of a temple complex."

3. Quoted by Vaughn Roberts in *God's Big Picture* (IVP, 2003), 52-53

4. Interestingly, according to Numbers 2-3, even the physical arrangement of the tabernacle and tribes was cruciform. When the nation was encamped in a particular location the tabernacle took center place, representing the nation's God-centered and God-dependent existence. The priestly Levites set up camp on the north, west, and south sides of the tabernacle while Moses, Aaron, and the priests camped on the east side by the entrance. The tents of the twelve tribes were then arranged evenly outside of the priests' tents; the four divisions of priests separated the tribes from the tabernacle itself, one division of priests per three tribes on each side of the tabernacle. When drawn out on a piece of paper, the cross-shaped arrangement of God's people is plainly seen.

5. In his excellent little book *God's Big Picture*, Vaughn Roberts

defines God's Kingdom as "God's people in God's place under God's rule and blessing," then follows that thread through the entire Bible.

6. G.K. Beale, *The Temple and the Church's Mission* (IVP, 2004), 402.

7. This does not mean, however, that believing women may not be called daughters of God. Paul calls them "daughters of God" in 2 Corinthians 6:16-18.

8. Jerry Bridges, *The Discipline of Grace* (NavPress, 1994), 124

9. Thanks to my friend Chuck DeBardeleben for developing this "two-way arrow" concept.

10. From Whitefield's sermon "The Method of Grace," http://www. reformed.org/documents/index.html?mainframe=/documents/ Whitefield/WITF_058.html (emphasis mine). Thanks to my friend Steve Williamson for supplying this quotation.

11. G. W. Barker, "1 John" in *The Expositor's Bible Commentary, Volume 12*, ed. F. E. Gaebelein (Zondervan, 1981), 346

12. *The ESV Study Bible*, 2532

13. I learned the acronym WIFE in seminary: the church, as Christ's bride or "WIFE," is marked by Worship, Instruction, Fellowship, and Evangelism (I use "expressions of service and witness" because it includes both evangelism and social justice ministry).

14. Portions of this chapter were originally published by and are used with the permission of BreakPoint.org: http://www. breakpoint.org/component/content/article/104-worldview- church/878-at-your-service

15. *Ibid.*

16. Thanks to T. M. Moore (www.ailbe.org) for teaching me the diakonos concept of serving God and others in our assigned "area of influence." I lean on his teaching in this chapter with his blessing.

17. John W. Fischer, *At Your Service* (Wiley & Sons, 2005), 79

18. Joseph R. Cooke, *Celebration of Grace* (Zondervan, 1991), 13 (emphasis mine).

19. Fischer, *op cit.* 17

20. Tim Keller writes profoundly about this parable in his best- selling book, *The Prodigal God* (Dutton, 2008). Read this great

book for much more depth than I am able to attempt here.

21. Two books that God used to powerfully teach me these concepts were John Piper's *Desiring God* (Multnomah, 2003) and Larry Crabb's *Inside Out* (NavPress, 2007). These books unpack the truth of Jeremiah 2:13 in different but transforming ways.

22. As quoted in "GospelTweets" (http://thegospelcoalition.org/blogs/tullian/2010/10/02/gospel-tweets).

23. Walter Marshall, *The Gospel Mystery of Sanctification*, revised into modern English by Bruce H. McRae (Wipf and Stock, 2005), 25-26.

24. I have rearranged the order of Pastor Marshall's "qualifications for living a godly life" to correspond to the order of the promises given in Ezekiel 36:25-28.

25. Marshall, *op cit.*, 29

26. Marshall, *op cit.*, 26

27. Marshall, *op cit.*, 36-38

28. This is the answer to *Westminster Shorter Catechism* Question 35, "What is sanctification?"

29. "The main promise of the covenant, which includes all others, is contained in the oft-repeated words, 'I will be a God unto thee and to thy seed after thee,' . . . This promise includes all others, such as the promise of temporal blessings, of justification, of the Spirit of God, and of final **glorification** in a life that never ends" (Louis Berkhof, *Summary of Christian Doctrine* [Banner of Truth, 1960], 82-83, emphasis mine).

30. In *Concise Theology*, J. I. Packer continues: "Paul's use of glory in 2 Corinthians 3:18 shows that for him sanctification of character is glorification begun. Then the physical transformation that gives us a body like Christ's, one that will match our totally transformed character and be a perfect means of expressing it, will be glorification completed (Philippians 3:20-21, 1 Corinthians 15:49-53)."

31. "For every one look at your sin, take ten looks at Christ" has been attributed to Robert Murray M'Cheyne. Richard Sibbes said, "There is more mercy in Christ than there is sin in me." I often use these two quotations to preach the gospel to myself and others.

32. C. S. Lewis, *Mere Christianity* (HarperCollins, 2001), 92

33. Jerry Bridges, *The Discipline of Grace* (NavPress, 1994), 128.

34. John Stott quoted by James C. Wilhoit in *Spiritual Formation as if the Church Mattered* (Baker, 2008), 39

35. Note on Galatians 3:5 in *The ESV Study Bible* (Crossway, 2008), 2249

36. Marshall, *op. cit.,* 183

37. Jerry Bridges, *The Discipline of Grace* (NavPress, 1994), 137

38. Larry said this during his School of Spiritual Direction, which you can learn more about at www.newwayministries.org.

39. Tim Keller, "The Gospel of Peace," a sermon on Philippians 4:4-13 given January 26, 2011, at Redeemer Seminary in Dallas, TX (http://audio.pcpc.org/archive/entry/5983).

40. Larry Crabb, *The PAPA Prayer: The Prayer You've Never Prayed* (Integrity, 2006), 10-11

41. Marshall, *op. cit.,* 204-205

42. *Ibid.,* 205-206

43. See T. M. Moore's *The Disciplines of Grace* (IVP, 2001)

44. Marshall, *op. cit.,* 224

45. John Piper, *When I Don't Desire God*, 91.

46. Adapted from "Walking Through Fire" in *From The Heart of a Lion*, (Bryan College Press, Dayton, TN, 2000).

47. Jerry Bridges, *Transforming Grace*

48. Larry Crabb defines "good enough Christianity" as what happens "when Christianity gets reduced to an opportunity to get the most out of life now and to become the happiest and healthiest and most fulfilled person you can be" (*66 Love Letters*, Thomas Nelson, 2010), xxv.

49. http://www.igracemusic.com/hymnbook/hymns/i09.html

50. *Desiring God*, 269-270

ABOUT CRUCIFORM PRESS

What would a book-publishing company for gospel-centered Christians look like if it began with the realities of 21st century technology?

We think It would focus on Content, Simplicity, Reliability, Trust, Convenience, Voice, and Community. Here's what we mean by that. These are our promises to you.

Content: Every book will be helpful, inspiring, biblical, and gospel-focused.

Simplicity: Every book will be short, clear, well-written, well-edited, and accessible.

Reliability: A new book will be released the first day of each month. Every book will be the same price. Each book will have a unique cover, yet all our books will maintain a distinctive, recognizable look.

Trust: If you like this book, then you're probably a lot like us in how you think, what you believe, and how you see the world. That means you can trust us to give you only the good stuff.

Convenience: Our books will be available in print, in a variety of ebook formats, and frequently as audiobooks. Print or ebook subscription opportunities can save you time and money.

Voice: We want to know what you'd like to read about, or who you think we ought to consider as an author, or really anything constructive you'd care to say about what we're doing and how we're doing it.

Community: We want to encourage and facilitate the sense of community that naturally exists among Christians who love the gospel of grace.

CruciformPress

Download our Free 109-page sampler

Download it at http://bit.ly/samplr